Major Muslim Nations

Afghanistan

Major Muslim Nations

Major Muslim Nations

Afghanistan

Dr. Kim Whitehead

Mason Crest Publishers
Philadelphia

Mason Crest Publishers
370 Reed Road
Broomall, PA 19008
www.masoncrest.com

First printing

1 3 5 7 9 8 6 4 2

Library of Congress Cataloging-in-Publication Data

Whitehead, Kim.
  Afghanistan / Kim Whitehead.
      p. cm. — (Major Muslim Nations)
    ISBN 978-1-4222-1403-9 (hardcover) — ISBN 978-1-4222-1433-6 (pbk.)
  1. Afghanistan—Juvenile literature. I. Title.
  DS351.5.W48 2005
  958.1—dc22

                            2008041241

Original ISBN: 1-59084-833-0 (hc)

Major Muslim Nations

Table of Contents

Dr. Harvey Sicherman, president and director of the Foreign Policy Research Institute, is the author of such books as *America the Vulnerable: Our Military Problems and How to Fix Them* (2002) and *Palestinian Autonomy, Self-Government and Peace* (1993).

Introduction

by Dr. Harvey Sicherman

America's triumph in the Cold War promised a new burst of peace and prosperity. Indeed, the decade between the demise of the Soviet Union and the destruction of September 11, 2001, seems in retrospect deceptively attractive. Today, of course, we are more fully aware—to our sorrow—of the dangers and troubles no longer just below the surface.

The Muslim identities of most of the terrorists at war with the United States have also provoked great interest in Islam and the role of religion in politics. A truly global religion, Islam's tenets are held by hundreds of millions of people from every ethnic group, scattered across the globe. It is crucial for Americans not to assume that Osama bin Laden's ideas are identical to those of most Muslims, or, for that matter, that most Muslims are Arabs. Also, it is important for Americans to understand the "hot spots" in the Muslim world because many will make an impact on the United States.

A glance at the map establishes the extraordinary coverage of our authors. Every climate and terrain may be found and every form of human society, from the nomads of the Central Asian steppes and Arabian deserts

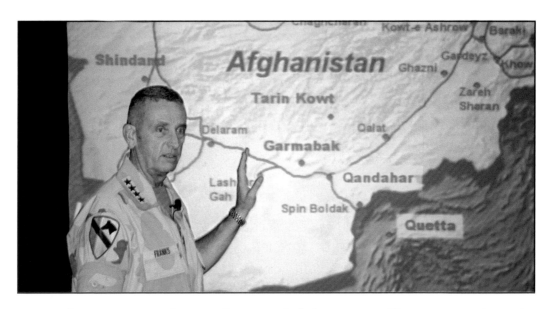

General Tommy Franks conducts a briefing on military operations in Afghanistan, November 2001. The United States led a coalition of allies into war against Afghanistan's Taliban government in the fall of 2001 because the Taliban was sheltering the al-Qaeda terrorist organization, responsible for the September 11 terrorist attacks on the World Trade Center and Pentagon.

to highly sophisticated cities such as Cairo and Singapore. Economies range from barter systems to stock exchanges, from oil-rich countries to the thriving semi-market powers, such as India, now on the march. Others have built wealth on service and shipping.

The Middle East and Central Asia are heavily armed and turbulent. Pakistan is a nuclear power, Iran threatens to become one, and Israel is assumed to possess a small arsenal. But in other places, such as Afghanistan and the Sudan, the horse and mule remain potent instruments of war. All have a rich history of conflict, domestic and international, old and new.

Governments include dictatorships, democracies, and hybrids without a name; centralized and decentralized administrations; and older patterns of tribal and clan associations. The region is a veritable encyclopedia of political expression.

Although such variety defies easy generalities, it is still possible to make several observations.

First, the regional geopolitics reflect the impact of empires and the struggles of post-imperial independence. While centuries-old history is often invoked, the truth is that the modern Middle East political system dates only from the 1920s, when the Ottoman Empire dissolved in the wake of its defeat by Britain and France in World War I. States such as Algeria, Iraq, Israel, Jordan, Kuwait, Saudi Arabia, Syria, Turkey, and the United Arab Emirates did not exist before 1914—they became independent between 1920 and 1971. Others, such as Egypt and Iran, were dominated by foreign powers until well after World War II. Few of the leaders of these states were happy with the territories they were assigned or the borders, which were often drawn by Europeans. Yet the system has endured despite many efforts to change it.

A similar story may be told in South Asia. The British Raj dissolved into India and Pakistan in 1947. Still further east, Malaysia shares a British experience but Indonesia, a Dutch invention, has its own European heritage. These imperial histories weigh heavily upon the politics of the region.

The second observation concerns economics, demography, and natural resources. These countries offer dramatic geographical contrasts: vast parched deserts and high mountains, some with year-round snow; stone-hard volcanic rifts and lush semi-tropical valleys; extremely dry and extremely wet conditions, sometimes separated by only a few miles; large permanent rivers and wadis, riverbeds dry as a bone until winter rains send torrents of flood from the mountains to the sea.

Although famous historically for its exports of grains, fabrics, and spices, most recently the Muslim regions are known more for a single commodity: oil. Petroleum is unevenly distributed; while it is largely concentrated in the Persian Gulf and Arabian Peninsula, large oil fields can be found in Algeria, Libya, and further east in Indonesia. Natural gas is also abundant in the

Gulf, and there are new, potentially lucrative offshore gas fields in the Eastern Mediterranean.

This uneven distribution of wealth has been compounded by demographics. Birth rates are very high, but the countries with the most oil are often lightly populated. Over the last decade, a youth "bulge" has emerged and this, combined with increased urbanization, has strained water supplies, air quality, public sanitation, and health services throughout the Muslim world. How will these young people be educated? Where will they work? A large outward migration, especially to Europe, indicates the lack of opportunity at home.

In the face of these challenges, the traditional state-dominated economic strategies have given way partly to experiments with "privatization" and foreign investment. But these have been very slow, and most people have yet to benefit from "globalization," although there are pockets of prosperity, high technology (notably Israel), and valuable natural resources (oil, gas, and minerals). Rising expectations have yet to be met.

A third important observation is the role of religion in the Middle East. Americans, who take separation of church and state for granted, should know that most countries in the region either proclaim their countries to be Muslim or allow a very large role for that religion in public life. (Islamic law, Shariah, permits people to practice Judaism and Christianity in Muslim states but only as *dhimmi*, protected but very second-class citizens.) Among those with predominantly Muslim populations, Turkey alone describes itself as secular and prohibits avowedly religious parties in the political system. Lebanon was a Christian-dominated state, and Israel continues to be a Jewish state. Even where politics are secular, religion plays an enormous role in culture, daily life, and legislation.

Islam has deeply affected every state and people in these regions. But Islamic practices and groups vary from the well-known Sunni and Shiite groups to energetic Salafi (Wahabi) and Sufi movements. Over the last 20

U.S. vice president Richard B. Cheney (left) shakes hands with Afghan leader Hamid Karzai at a press conference, December 7, 2004. Earlier that day, Karzai had been sworn in as Afghanistan's first president under a new constitution.

years especially, South and Central Asia have become battlegrounds for competing Shiite (Iranian) and Wahabi (Saudi) doctrines, well financed from abroad and aggressively antagonistic toward non-Muslims and each other. Resistance to the Soviet war in Afghanistan brought these groups battle-tested warriors and organizers responsive to the doctrines made popular by Osama bin Laden and others. This newly significant struggle within Islam, superimposed on an older Muslim history, will shape political and economic destinies throughout the region and beyond.

We hope that these books will enlighten both teacher and student about the critical "hot spots" of the Muslim world. These countries would be important in their own right to Americans; arguably, after 9/11, they became vital to our national security. And the enduring impact of Islam is a crucial factor we must understand. We at the Foreign Policy Research Institute hope these books will illuminate both the facts and the prospects.

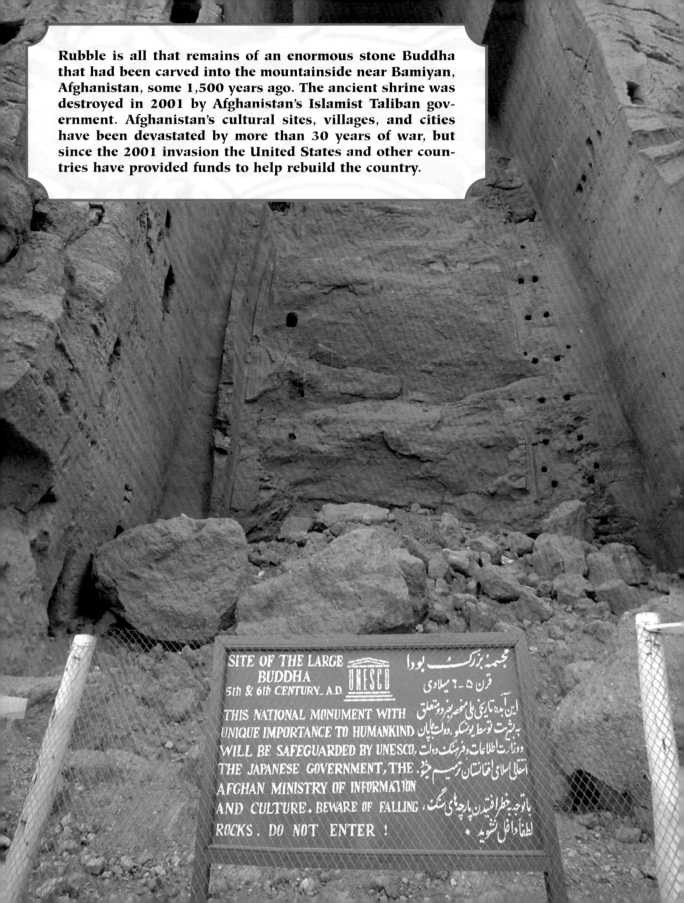

Rubble is all that remains of an enormous stone Buddha that had been carved into the mountainside near Bamiyan, Afghanistan, some 1,500 years ago. The ancient shrine was destroyed in 2001 by Afghanistan's Islamist Taliban government. Afghanistan's cultural sites, villages, and cities have been devastated by more than 30 years of war, but since the 2001 invasion the United States and other countries have provided funds to help rebuild the country.

SITE OF THE LARGE BUDDHA 5th & 6th CENTURY A.D. UNESCO

THIS NATIONAL MONUMENT WITH UNIQUE IMPORTANCE TO HUMANKIND WILL BE SAFEGUARDED BY UNESCO, THE JAPANESE GOVERNMENT, THE AFGHAN MINISTRY OF INFORMATION AND CULTURE. BEWARE OF FALLING ROCKS. DO NOT ENTER!

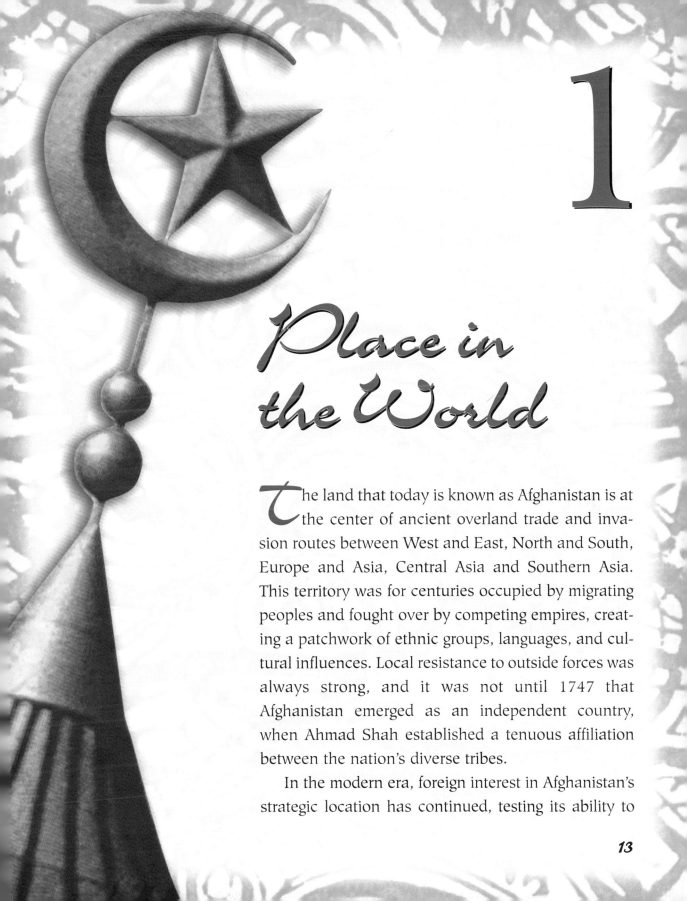

1

Place in the World

*T*he land that today is known as Afghanistan is at the center of ancient overland trade and invasion routes between West and East, North and South, Europe and Asia, Central Asia and Southern Asia. This territory was for centuries occupied by migrating peoples and fought over by competing empires, creating a patchwork of ethnic groups, languages, and cultural influences. Local resistance to outside forces was always strong, and it was not until 1747 that Afghanistan emerged as an independent country, when Ahmad Shah established a tenuous affiliation between the nation's diverse tribes.

In the modern era, foreign interest in Afghanistan's strategic location has continued, testing its ability to remain unified and sovereign. During the 19th century, the country's current borders were drawn amid struggles over the region between Great Britain and Russia; and in the 20th century it was influenced by both the United States and the Soviet Union (and ultimately occupied by the latter).

More recently, Afghanistan became the focus of international attention as the country's strict Islamic Taliban government provided safe haven for the terrorist network al-Qaeda, the chief suspect in the September 2001 attacks on New York and Washington, D.C. Since a U.S.-led coalition ousted the Taliban in late 2001, pictures and news stories from Afghanistan have focused on the country's devastation by long years of warfare and its ethnic conflicts, but an in-depth look at Afghanistan's rich history and cultural practices reveals a much more complex and fascinating place.

National Character

Afghanistan's diverse ethnic groups have shown unity particularly when threatened by foreign invaders. In addition to being farmers, artisans, and nomads, Afghans are expert warriors. Afghan resistance to the Soviet occupation of their land (1979–1989) ended with the retreat of one of the world's superpowers.

Another key factor in Afghans' shared national identity is their devotion to Islam, the monotheistic religion established by the prophet Muhammad on the Arabian Peninsula in the seventh century. Islam was the dominant religion of Central Asia by the ninth century, and for more than a thousand years Islamic beliefs and celebrations, as well as adherence to Islamic laws, have served as unifying factors among Afghan ethnic groups. Islam has also informed Afghans' affinity for beauty; their mosques are topped with elaborate domes, minarets, and intricate tile work.

Along with the influence of Islam, other common factors among Afghans include strong extended families, a largely agricultural way of life, a deep love of poetry and folktales, and generous hospitality to strangers.

The Promise of the Future

Afghanistan was ruled by a monarchy from 1747 to 1973, by Afghan Communists and Soviet occupiers in the 1970s and 1980s, and by an alliance of resistance fighters (*mujahedin*) and then the Taliban in the 1990s. From 1979 to 2001, extensive fighting occurred throughout the country, first between Soviet forces and the Afghan resistance and then between rival internal factions struggling for control. Since the Taliban was defeated in 2001, the country has been working with the United Nations (U.N.) to establish a new and democratic government.

Now Afghanistan stands at a crossroads, poised between the devastation caused by warfare and the possibility of a brighter political and economic future. More than 20 years of conflict have resulted in crushing poverty, a landscape riddled with land mines (up to 10 million, according to U.N. statistics), and vast destruction of the country's roads, housing, public buildings, education and health care systems, and historical and artistic treasures. The nation also faces numerous other challenges: rival **warlords** retain power in different regions of the country, terrorist groups continue to operate in remote mountain regions, and the level of international aid lags significantly behind the needs of the population.

But Afghan refugees are returning home after years of exile and tenaciously reviving their farms, businesses, and modes of cultural and artistic expression. And as Afghans undertake yet another transformation of their national institutions, they are attempting to embrace a democratic model of government without sacrificing their dedication to Islamic principles.

Their work to renew their country is an extension of that of Ahmad Shah, the man who first united Afghanistan's tribes and wrote of the land he loved in the poem "Love of a Nation":

> If I must choose between the world and you,
>
> I shall not hesitate to claim your barren deserts as my own.

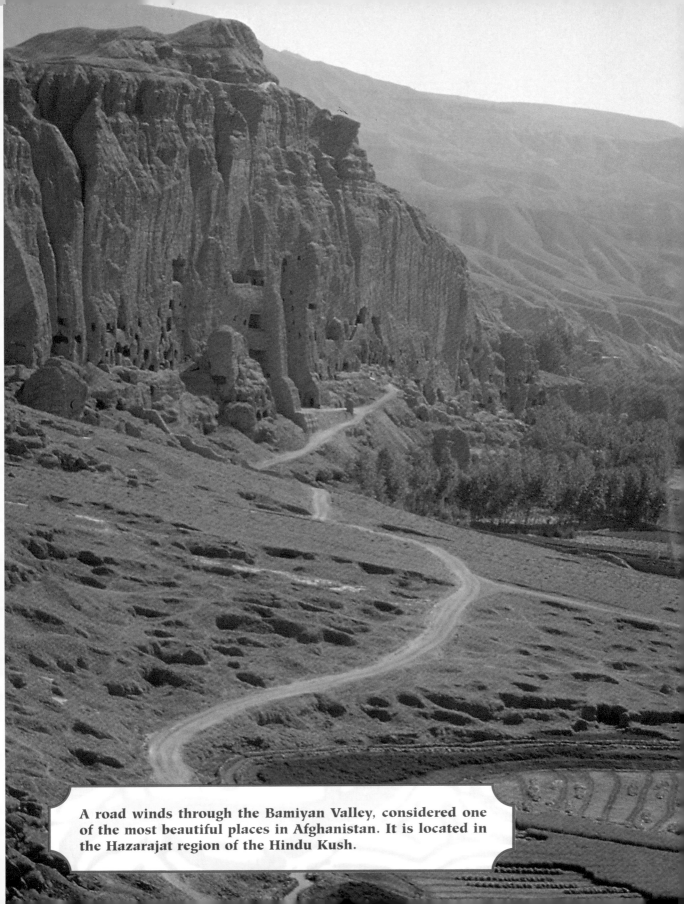

A road winds through the Bamiyan Valley, considered one of the most beautiful places in Afghanistan. It is located in the Hazarajat region of the Hindu Kush.

2

The Land

One key to Afghans' fierce resistance to invaders has been their deep familiarity with the harsh landscape of their country. Mountains run like a spine through Afghanistan from the northeast to the southwest, dominating the landscape. Rolling plains and grasslands stretch across northern Afghanistan, while fertile mountain valleys dot the east, and deserts extend through the west and southwest. Much of the terrain is rugged, and the climate is marked by seasonal extremes.

Afghanistan is a landlocked nation shaped roughly like a leaf. It is approximately the size of Texas, with a total area of 250,000 square miles (647,500 square kilometers). Afghanistan is bordered by six countries. To the north lie its Central Asian neighbors Tajikistan, Uzbekistan, and Turkmenistan, and high in the Pamir Mountains to the northeast runs a short border with

China. Afghanistan's longest borders are with Pakistan on the east and south and Iran to the west.

Only 12 percent of Afghanistan is **arable**, and less than 10 percent of the country is actually used for growing crops. Farming is limited to small areas of land that can be irrigated and to some northern areas that receive above-average rainfall. The rest is mountains, many covered permanently with snow, and desert. Grasslands can be found throughout the country, however, and up to 70 percent of Afghanistan's land can be used for grazing livestock.

Afghanistan contains three regions: the central highlands, with their towering mountain peaks; the northern plains, which are heavily farmed and densely populated; and the southwestern plateau, which includes mostly desert.

The Central Highlands

The central highlands are dominated by tall mountains and deep, narrow valleys. The highest of the mountain ranges in this region is the Hindu Kush, which has historically played a key role in the defense of the country. The Hindu Kush is considered by most geographers to be the westernmost section of the Pamir, Karakorum, and Himalaya mountain ranges. It extends a total of 500 miles (805 kilometers) through parts of Afghanistan, Pakistan, and Tajikistan. Though the origins of the name remain a mystery, Hindu Kush translates as "Hindu killer."

The Hindu Kush forms a natural barrier between the fertile northern plains and the rest of the country. The mountains in eastern Afghanistan act as obstacles to the winds that carry moisture from the Indian Ocean, and this causes the dry climate of most of the country.

The Hindu Kush includes two dozen peaks that rise more than 23,000 feet (7,010 meters). The highest is Nowshak, at 24,557 feet (7,485 meters). The mountains of the Hindu Kush range decrease in height as they stretch

The Geography of Afghanistan

Location: Southern Asia, north and west of Pakistan, east of Iran

Area: slightly smaller than Texas
    total: 250,000 square miles (647,500 sq km)
    land: 250,000 square miles (647,500 sq km)
    water: 0 square miles

Borders: Pakistan, 1,510 miles (2,430 km); Tajikistan, 749 miles (1,206 km); Iran, 582 miles (936 km); Turkmenistan, 462 miles (744 km); Uzbekistan, 85 miles (137 km); China, 47 miles (76 km)

Climate: arid to semiarid, with cold winters and hot summers

Terrain: mostly rugged mountains, with plains in north and southwest

Elevation extremes:
    lowest point: Amu Darya—846 feet (258 meters)
    highest point: Nowshak—24,557 feet (7,485 meters)

Natural hazards: damaging earthquakes in the Hindu Kush mountains; flooding; droughts

Source: Adapted from CIA World Factbook, 2008.

westward: near the middle, close to the country's capital, Kabul, they reach 20,000 feet (6,000 meters), while farther to the west the peaks reach 11,500 feet (3,500 meters). The average altitude of the range is 14,700 feet (4,481 meters).

Snowfall is heavy in the Hindu Kush, and meltwater feeds the Amu Darya and Indus Rivers. Little vegetation grows at the higher elevations in the mountains, but the valleys are irrigated and densely populated. The lower mountain slopes contain a diversity of trees and wildlife, but extensive logging and warfare have significantly damaged the mountain forests.

Several high-altitude mountain passes provide a way over the Hindu Kush and have long been important for passage by caravans. These were used by Alexander the Great, the Mughal emperor Babur, and others as passageways to India, but are now trade routes. Most of the passes rise between 12,000 and 15,000 feet (3,658 and 4,572 meters), and all are closed by snow six months out of the year. The most important have been the Shebar Pass, located northwest of Kabul, and the Khyber Pass, which leads to the Indian subcontinent. The Hindu Kush mountains divide the northern provinces from the rest of the country, and in 1964 the Soviets constructed a tunnel below the Salang Pass, greatly reducing travel time between Kabul and northern Afghanistan.

From the Hindu Kush, lower ranges radiate in all directions, including the Pamirs in the upper northeast (known as the Wakhan Corridor), the Badakhshan Ranges in the northeast, the Paropamisus Range in the north, and the Safed Koh along the border between Afghanistan and Pakistan. As the mountains stretch further west and south, they gradually get smaller and spread out into central Afghanistan as dusty hills.

Around 50 earthquakes are recorded each year in Afghanistan. The most severe in recent history occurred in 1985 and measured 7.3 on the Richter scale. More recently, in March 2002 an earthquake in the Hindu Kush mountains killed approximately 2,000 people and left another 20,000 homeless. The epicenter of most earthquakes lies in the northeastern central highlands.

The Northern Plains

The northern plains run north of the central highlands and include roughly 40,000 square miles (103,600 sq km) of fertile foothills and plains. They are part of the very large Central Asian **steppe** and stretch from near Afghanistan's border with Tajikistan westward toward the Iranian border. The average elevation is about 2,000 feet (610 meters).

Farming predominates in the northern plains, and the region is densely populated. The Amu Darya River (formerly called the Oxus) and its two most significant tributaries, the Kokcha and Kunduz, are fed by snow runoff from the Hindu Kush. Rainfall is inadequate, however, so farming occurs only in river valleys and where the land can be irrigated. The northern plains are also home to rich mineral deposits, especially of natural gas and oil.

The Southwestern Plateau

The southwestern plateau is separated from the northern plains by the Hindu Kush. Consisting mainly of high plateaus, sandy deserts, and semi-deserts, the region covers about 50,000 square miles (129,500 sq km) and averages 3,000 feet (914 meters) above sea level. The southwestern plateau is bisected by the Helmand River. South of the Helmand lies the Registan Desert, which covers one-fourth to one-third of the region. North of the river is the Dasht-i-Margo Desert, which is dominated by salt flats and desolate plains, and the Dasht-i-Khash Desert. Lake Helmand, one of only a few lakes in the entire country, is also found in the region. The marshland known as Gaud-i-Zirreh is located in the extreme southwest. The soil throughout the region is very infertile, except along the rivers.

Lakes and Rivers

The four major river systems in Afghanistan are the Amu Darya (which forms much of the border with Central Asia), the Helmand, the Harirud, and the Kabul. In the country's arid climate, many rivers and streams empty through evaporation, while some flow only during rainy seasons. The Amu Darya, Helmand, and Harirud are all used for agricultural irrigation. The country's capital is located on the Kabul River, which flows through gorges north of the Khyber Pass and joins the Indus River system in Pakistan.

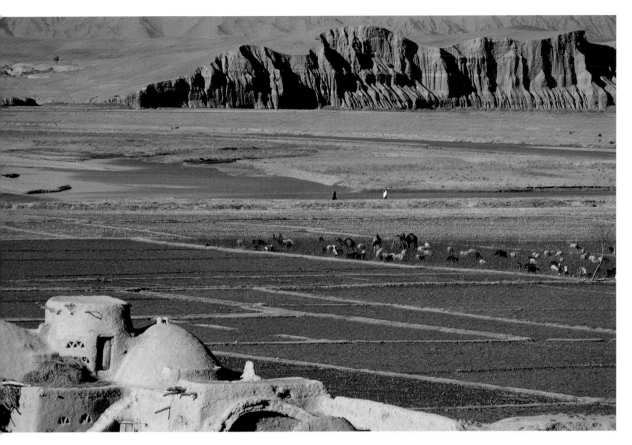

Beyond this ancient mud-brick building complex are the green fields of the Helmand River valley.

Three major dams have been constructed on Afghanistan's rivers: the Arghandab Dam on a tributary of the Helmand River above Kandahar, the Naglu Dam on the Kabul River, and the Kajakai Dam on the Helmand River. All are in need of repair because of a lack of maintenance during Afghanistan's recent conflicts.

The country's longest river is the Helmand, which flows from the Hindu Kush Mountains all the way into Iran, where it then empties into a series of landlocked lakes along the Afghanistan-Iran border. During the latest drought, Afghanistan released very little water through the Helmand Dam, turning the area along its border with Iran into a desert.

Climate

The climate of Afghanistan is arid to semiarid. Precipitation averages only about 7 inches annually and occurs mainly as winter snowfall at higher elevations. A record 53 inches (1.3 meters) has been recorded at the Salang Pass in the Hindu Kush, while some areas in western Afghanistan receive only about 3 inches a year.

The four seasons are distinct in Afghanistan. Summers are hot and dry everywhere, except on the highest mountains. The country's scant rainfall arrives in spring and autumn. Winters are cold and generally snowy, especially in mountain areas. In the Hindu Kush on the border with Pakistan, the snow is frequently more than six feet (two meters) deep during the winter.

Temperatures can be harsh, from the arctic winter conditions of the mountains to the extremely hot summers of lowland areas. Temperatures range from −20° Fahrenheit (−29° Celsius) in the mountains to 120°F (49°C) in the deserts. Daytime and nighttime temperatures can also vary dramatically. For example, summer daytime temperatures in the deserts climb to 120°F (49°C), but drop below freezing at night.

Some eastern areas bordering Pakistan are affected by the monsoon, but it does not reach the southwest or the north. A strong wind called the *Bad-i-sad-o-bist* ("wind of 120 days") blows through the south and west during the summer months, bringing intense heat, drought, and sandstorms. Winter blizzards are also common in the Sistan Basin.

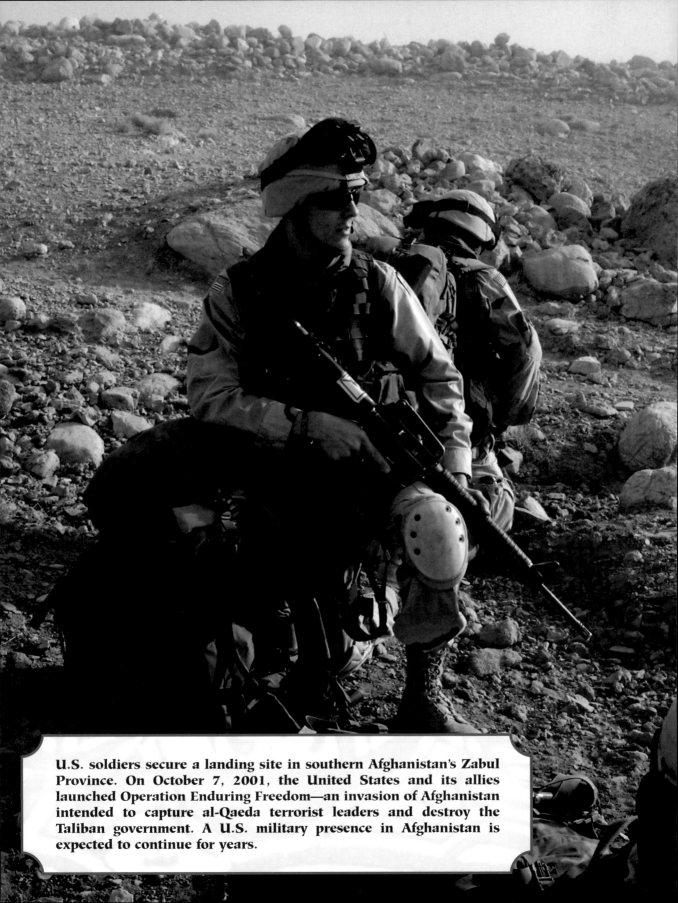

U.S. soldiers secure a landing site in southern Afghanistan's Zabul Province. On October 7, 2001, the United States and its allies launched Operation Enduring Freedom—an invasion of Afghanistan intended to capture al-Qaeda terrorist leaders and destroy the Taliban government. A U.S. military presence in Afghanistan is expected to continue for years.

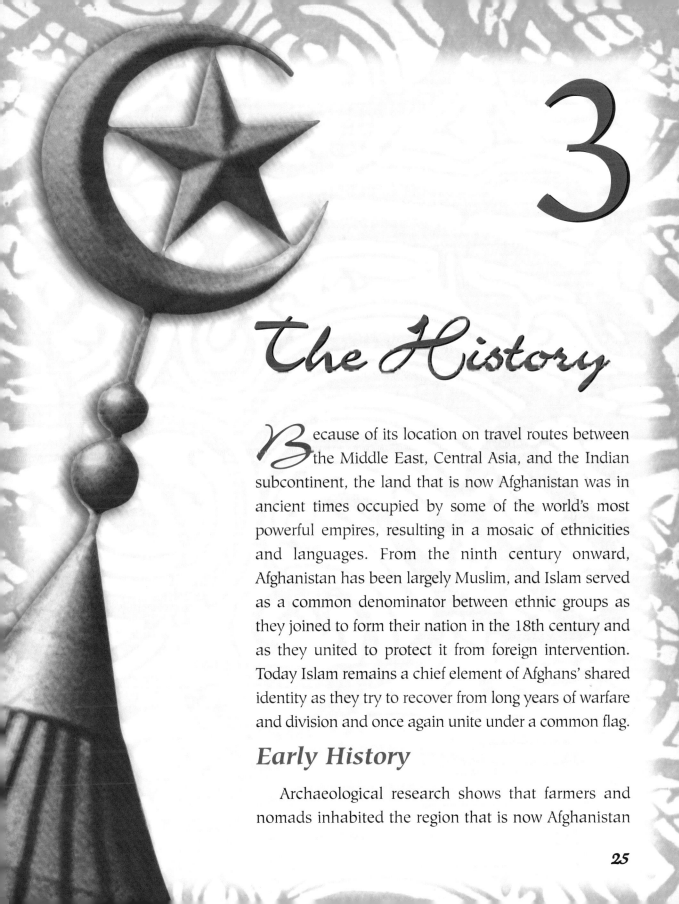

3

The History

Because of its location on travel routes between the Middle East, Central Asia, and the Indian subcontinent, the land that is now Afghanistan was in ancient times occupied by some of the world's most powerful empires, resulting in a mosaic of ethnicities and languages. From the ninth century onward, Afghanistan has been largely Muslim, and Islam served as a common denominator between ethnic groups as they joined to form their nation in the 18th century and as they united to protect it from foreign intervention. Today Islam remains a chief element of Afghans' shared identity as they try to recover from long years of warfare and division and once again unite under a common flag.

Early History

Archaeological research shows that farmers and nomads inhabited the region that is now Afghanistan as early as 10,000 years ago. By 6000 B.C.E., the semiprecious stone lapis lazuli was being exported from northeastern Afghanistan to India, a sign of early trade to and from the region.

Greek soldiers of Alexander the Great stop to examine a burning seep of natural gas in Bactria, in the northern part of modern-day Afghanistan. Alexander introduced Greek culture to the region in the fourth century B.C.E.

In the sixth century B.C.E., the Achaemenid dynasty of Persia extended its rule east to the Indus River, which flows through what is today Pakistan. The religion called **Zoroastrianism** flourished under Persian rule—legend has it that Zoroaster himself was born and lived in the Afghan region known as Bactria in the fifth century B.C.E. The Persian rulers Cyrus the Great and Darius the Great were followed by the Macedonian ruler Alexander the Great, who brought Greek culture and founded cities throughout the region in the fourth century B.C.E., and by the Mauryan (Indian) dynasty, which brought Buddhism to the region. Throughout this period, nomadic tribes rebelled against the ruling empires.

The region was next occupied by waves of people migrating out of Central Asia. The most influential of these were the Kushans, who encouraged trade along the

Silk Road. This was the name for a network of trade routes that stretched 4,000 miles (6,437 km) between China and the Mediterranean, crossing the Hindu Kush mountains in the process. Under the Kushans, Buddhism held sway, though Greek influence continued to be strong as well.

The Kushans ruled until the third century C.E., when they lost ground to the Persian Sassanid dynasty and another wave of migrants, the Ephthalites (White Huns), who were in turn overcome by the Sassanids and the Turkish tribes of Central Asia in the sixth century C.E.

Islamic Rule

The monotheistic religion known as Islam first came to Afghanistan in the seventh century, not long after the death of the religion's central human figure, the prophet Muhammad. Muhammad ibn Abdallah (ca. 570–632) was a shepherd and caravan merchant who lived in the town of Mecca on the Arabian Peninsula (present-day Saudi Arabia). In 610 C.E., when Muhammad was about 40 years old, he received a series of revelations from God, which were later compiled into the Qur'an (also spelled Koran), the sacred text of Islam. Muhammad preached against social inequality and **polytheism**, which pitted him against the powerful tribal leaders in Mecca. After he and his followers were forced to leave Mecca in

The Silk Road was an ancient network of trade routes and trading posts that extended several thousand miles between China and the Mediterranean Sea. The land that is now Afghanistan lay in the "crossroads" region of the most important branch of the Silk Road, and the ancient city of Balkh was a key stopping point for the caravans carrying silk, spices, furs, gold, precious stones, and textiles.

622, Muhammad established an Islamic government in the Arabian oasis town of Medina. Over the next few years, Muhammad's teachings attracted greater numbers of followers, and by 630 the Muslims were strong enough to return to Mecca and take control of its holy shrine, the Kaaba, which became a center for Muslim pilgrimage.

The religion continued to grow after the death of Muhammad in 632, and Arab armies soon spread Islam far beyond the Arabian Peninsula. Within 100 years, the Islamic religious state had conquered the Persian Empire and spread as far east as the Great Wall of China and as far west as northern Africa and the Iberian Peninsula of western Europe.

Afghanistan quickly became part of the Muslim empire. In 651,

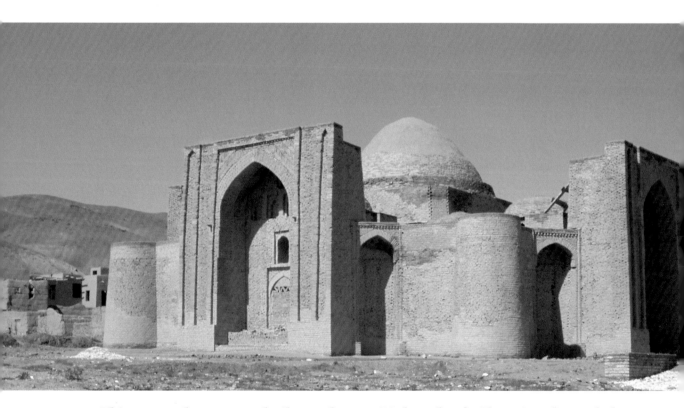

This mausoleum was built to honor Mahmud of Ghazni, who ruled Afghanistan from 998 to 1030. During his reign, many people converted to Islam.

Muslim Arabs conquered the towns of Herat and Balkh, in present-day western Afghanistan. By the ninth century, most inhabitants of what are now Afghanistan, Pakistan, Central Asia, and northern India were converted to **Sunni** Islam. Among the greatest leaders in Afghanistan during this period was Mahmud, who ruled from 998 until 1030 and oversaw mass conversions to Islam and a cultural flourishing in the city of Ghazni.

For hundreds of years, the Afghanistan region was, at least nominally, under the control of the Arab Islamic empire. This vast empire was ruled from Baghdad by the Abbasid **caliphate**. But in the 13th century Abbasid control was shaken by the arrival of a new power from the east: the Mongols. In 1220, under the command of Genghis Khan (ca. 1162–1227), the Mongols swept through Central Asia from China and massacred the populations of entire cities in Afghanistan. The Mongols also destroyed much of the sophisticated **karez** irrigation system that kept portions of the country green and prosperous, turning lush valleys into barren deserts.

After the death of Genghis Khan, the Mongols continued to press west. By 1258 a Mongol army under one of Genghis's grandsons, Hulegü Khan, sacked Baghdad, destroying the Abbasid dynasty. By 1260 the Mongols controlled a vast area of Asia that stretched from China to the eastern Mediterranean Sea. However, the Mongols would not be able to maintain the unity of their empire, as internal struggles for leadership caused it to fragment into four separate groups, based in China, Central Asia, Russia, and western Asia. The Mongol empire in Central Asia was known as the Chagatai Khanate, after one of Genghis Khan's sons, who had been granted control over the region after Genghis's death.

Although the Mongols had destroyed the Arab Islamic empire, Islam remained a powerful and influential force. By 1300 many of the Mongol conquerors had converted to the religion. When a Mongol named Tarmashirin became ruler of the Chagatai Khanate in 1326, he made Islam the official state religion.

The Chagatai Khanate was arguably the weakest of the Mongol empires because it was the smallest. At various points in the 14th century it was under the influence of the other khanates. But by the end of the century a new leader who hoped to reunite the enormous empire of Genghis Khan and his sons had emerged. By 1400 the Turkic Mongol Timur Lenk (Timur the Lame) ruled all of Afghanistan and northern India. A brutal ruler, Timur (ca. 1336–1405) made piles from the skulls of his enemies as memorials to his conquests. Nevertheless, he turned the capital, Samarkand (in what is now Uzbekistan), into a political and cultural center. After his death, his son led a cultural renaissance in Herat, promoting architecture, literature, music, and the visual arts.

Although Timur had attempted to create a Central Asian empire, he did not establish a bureaucracy that could govern the vast territory after his death. His descendants held power over the Afghanistan region until the 1500s, when the Persian Safavid dynasty extended its influence north into the country. The Safavids established **Shia** Islam as the official religion of Persia. Their only rival in Afghanistan was the Mughal dynasty, founded by Babur ("the Tiger"), a descendant of Timur; the Mughals conquered and ruled India. During the next century and a half, the two empires battled for control over Central Asia.

The struggle between the Safavids and the Mughals continued until the emergence of the Persian warrior Nadir Shah (1688–1747). He defeated the Afghans, who had assumed control over parts of Persia, then overthrew the last Persian Safavid ruler and installed a puppet on the throne. Nadir Shah then advanced against the Afghans and the Mughal Empire, conquering Kabul and Kandahar in 1738 and sacking Delhi the next year. This ended Mughal control over Afghanistan and signaled the decline of the Mughal Empire. Nadir Shah was successful in his effort to create a new Persian empire—he is considered one of the greatest Persian rulers—but his empire disintegrated soon after his assassination in 1747.

The Birth of Afghanistan

After Nadir Shah's death a man named Ahmad, who was a member of the large Pashtun ethnic group and who had served as a military leader under Nadir Shah, persuaded the disparate Afghan tribes to assert their independence and appoint him their *amir*, or leader. He adopted the title "Durr-i-Durrani" ("pearl of pearls") and changed the name of his Pashtun clan from the Abdali to the Durrani. Within 10 years, his forces took control of all of Afghanistan and portions of Central Asia and India, establishing a Durrani empire. Though he eventually lost control of some of the lands he had conquered, he was the first to unify the tribes of present-day Afghanistan, and he is known today as Ahmad Shah Baba—the Father of Afghanistan.

After Ahmad Shah's death in 1772, a series of inept rulers held the throne, causing tension and even open warfare among Afghanistan's tribes. A powerful tribal chief named Painda Khan established alliances with other tribes that enabled him to place

Persian ruler Nadir Shah (1688–1747) invaded Afghanistan in 1738, shifting control over the territory from the declining Mughal Empire of India to his resurgent Persian Empire. After his assassination, the Afghan tribes united under the leadership of Ahmad Shah Baba and gained independence from Persia.

his son Mahmud on the throne from 1800 to 1803, but Mahmud was replaced by the son of another tribal chief, Shah Shuja, from 1803 to 1809.

In June 1809 Shuja signed a treaty of friendship with Great Britain—Afghanistan's first formal agreement with a foreign country. At the time the British were trying to conquer the Indian subcontinent and wanted to shield their new possessions from a potential Russian threat. Shah Shuja promised that he would not permit foreign troops to pass through Afghanistan to attack the British in India, while the British agreed to prevent Persian forces from invading Afghanistan.

A few weeks after signing the treaty, Shuja's government was overthrown, and he fled to British India. Mahmud again took power over Afghanistan, but continuing tribal disagreements led to unrest and violence. The situation became even worse after Mahmud's death in 1818, as the country fragmented. "Chaos reigned in the domains of Ahmad Shah Durrani's empire as various sons of Painda Khan struggled for supremacy," writes Craig Baxter in *Afghanistan: A Country Study*. "Afghanistan ceased to exist as a single nation, disintegrating for a brief time into a fragmented collection of small units, each ruled by a different Durrani leader."

A Buffer Between Russia and British India

In 1826 Amir Dost Muhammad, a descendant of Painda Khan, came to the throne. This brought some stability back to Afghanistan, but his reign also marked the beginning of intervention in the country by Britain and Russia, as they faced off in what became known as "the Great Game." The British, who at this point were still engaged in the conquest of India, worried about a Russian invasion using routes from Central Asia through Afghanistan. In turn, the Russians feared that the British would expand their control northward into Central Asia, which they regarded as their sphere of interest.

In 1836, after losing control of Peshawar to the **Sikh** ruler Ranjit Singh, Dost Muhammad turned to the British for help. The British, however, were

This 19th-century drawing shows Dost Muhammad surrendering to the British commander, Sir William Macnaghten, at the entrance to Kabul in the fall of 1840. The British allowed Dost Muhammad to leave Afghanistan for exile in India. He returned in 1843, after the British withdrew from Afghanistan, and ruled until 1863.

more interested in helping the ruler of Herat, who in 1837 tried to resist a Persian siege assisted by the Russians. Having failed to receive British help, Dost Muhammad turned to the Russians. This led to the First Anglo-Afghan War (1838–1842), which began with the British invasion of Kandahar and Kabul, to reinstall the former Shah Shuja. The superior British military won decisive victories, and Dost Muhammad, betrayed by the Russians, fled Afghanistan in 1839.

In 1840 Dost Muhammad reentered the country to lead the Afghan tribes against the British occupying force and the puppet king in a nation-wide insurrection. Although the British eventually captured Dost Muhammad, his son Akbar Khan completed the rout of the British invaders. When the British tried to withdraw from Kabul to Jalalabad, they were massacred by tribal warriors. Of the 16,000 British troops and dependents in the Kabul garrison, only one man reached Jalalabad safely.

In 1843 the British released Dost Muhammad and allowed him to return to Afghanistan, where he again assumed the throne. The British ini-

This photo of a British camp in Afghanistan was taken in 1879, during the Second Anglo-Afghan War. Afghanistan was an important piece in the Great Game, a decades-long imperial struggle between Great Britain and Russia. Throughout the 19th century, as the Russian Empire aggressively expanded into Central Asia, British leaders feared that India, Britain's prize colony, might eventually be vulnerable to Russian invasion. In order to create a buffer state that would forestall that possibility, the British inserted themselves into Afghanistan.

tially refused to deal with him, but during the 1840s and 1850s, the relationship gradually grew warmer. In 1855 the two countries signed the Treaty of Peshawar, which made them allies. The British also allowed Dost Muhammad to consolidate his rule by occupying Kandahar (1855), Balkh (1859), and Herat (1863).

After Dost Muhammad's death in 1863, his son Sher Ali Khan became the ruler. Relations between Sher Ali Khan and the British deteriorated over the next 15 years. In the late 1860s the Russians conquered much of Turkestan, thereby extending their military control to Afghanistan's northern border along the Amu Darya River. The British grew further alarmed when, in 1878, the Afghan amir signed a treaty with Russia; earlier the amir had rejected a British offer. This led to the Second Anglo-Afghan War (1878–1880). The Afghans did not receive the help they had hoped for from Russia, and in the end they were defeated. To get the British occupying army out of the country, the Afghans had to permit a permanent British embassy in Kabul, which was to supervise the conduct of their foreign relations and pay a regular yearly allowance in hard cash to the obedient Afghan ruler.

After a short reign by Sher Ali's son Yaqub, his nephew Abdur Rahman Khan was allowed by the British to return from exile in Bukhara to become the new ruler. In two decades of rule (1880–1901), he established control over the tribes, initiated modernization efforts, and divided the country into provinces, in which governors enforced laws irrespective of tribal customs. Abdur Rahman established a national army and brought many European experts to the country, including doctors, engineers, and irrigation specialists. He was also the first ruler to call a *loya jirga*, an assembly of tribal and religious leaders, though they did little more than rubber-stamp his proposals.

Although the British had backed the ascension of Abdur Rahman to the Afghan throne, tensions with Britain continued during his reign, this time over the Pashtun lands in eastern Afghanistan. In 1893 Abdur Rahman reluctantly agreed with the British to establish a boundary—the so-called Durand Line—between British India and Afghanistan that cut through the Pashtun territory (often referred to as Pashtunistan). Although the Durand Line was never intended to become a *de jure* international boundary, it has turned into one. A permanent source of both friction and stability, it has remained unchanged to the present day, forming the boundary between Afghanistan and Pakistan.

The 20th Century: Independence and Instability

Abdur Rahman's son Habibullah took the throne peacefully after his father's death in 1901. Afghan **nationalism** grew during Habibullah's reign, and he developed closer ties to Western countries, a move criticized by Muslim leaders. Meanwhile, the Great Game ended in 1907 with the signing of the Anglo-Russian Convention. Under this agreement Russia agreed not to expand into Afghanistan, while Britain promised not to meddle in the country's internal affairs. Afghanistan was to be a neutral country, and it remained neutral during World War I (1914–1918) despite pressure from the Muslim Ottoman Empire to enter the war on the side of the Central Powers (which included Germany and Austria-Hungary) against Great Britain, Russia, and their European allies. The Anglo-Russian Convention remained in force until the 1917 overthrow of czarist rule and the eventual rise to power of the Bolsheviks, who established the Union of Soviet Socialist Republics in 1922, after a period of civil war in Russia.

Political leadership was unstable in Afghanistan throughout the 20th century. From 1919 until 1973, when the monarchy was abolished, 11 Afghan kings were assassinated, executed, or forcibly removed from power.

After the assassination of Habibullah in 1919, his third son, Amanullah, took the throne. Several weeks later Amanullah, hoping that

Amanullah Khan salutes as he walks through Berlin with German president Paul von Hindenberg, 1926. After Amanullah became the ruler of Afghanistan in 1919, he gained greater control over his country's international affairs and implemented internal reforms.

the Russian Bolsheviks would come to support him, started a military campaign against the British, known as the Third Anglo-Afghan War (1919). Although Bolshevik help did not arrive, the British, being pressed elsewhere, offered Amanullah a deal, which he accepted with the proviso that the Afghans gain the right to conduct their own foreign affairs. This was the Treaty of Rawalpindi, which was amended in 1921.

Now that Afghanistan was free to pursue its own foreign policy, it established relations with major countries around the world. In 1921 Afghanistan became the first country to recognize the Bolshevik government of the Soviet Union. Afghanistan therefore became the beneficiary of a "special relationship" with the U.S.S.R., but one that would ultimately turn sour.

As king of Afghanistan, Amanullah instituted radical constitutional, administrative, and educational reforms in many areas of Afghan life. He actively promoted Western educational models, introduced a national tax system, and modernized his military. Amanullah also encouraged people to wear Western clothing, and he wanted to "free" Afghan women by trying to end the traditional Islamic practices of veiling and seclusion. These reforms offended religious and tribal leaders, who insisted that Islamic law (*Sharia*) remain the law of the land.

In 1928 a civil war broke out. This time the Soviets offered to assist Amanullah but sent only weak forces that never crossed the Hindu Kush. The following year Amanullah abdicated. This satisfied the British, who were suspicious of his swift reforms. They offered him passage into exile, from which he was never to return. (He died in 1960 in Zurich, Switzerland.)

In the chaos that followed, a Tajik rebel leader named Bachah Saqow ("the son of a water carrier") surrounded Kabul and proclaimed himself amir. This was too much for the Pashtun tribesmen. Headed by Mohammad Nadir Khan, a distant cousin of Amanullah who had been a military leader during the Third Anglo-Afghan War, they took control of Kabul. Bachah Saqow was captured and executed in November 1929, and Nadir Khan became the new king of Afghanistan.

In 1931 Nadir Khan introduced a new constitution to appease the religious leaders. Though the constitution emphasized the Sharia, the king quietly continued modernizing the country, improving roads and communications, building the army, and establishing commercial relationships with foreign countries. He also restored unity to Afghanistan while strengthening the clannish foundations of his rule.

Nadir Khan was assassinated in 1933. He was succeeded by his 19-year-old son, Zahir Shah, who would rule for 40 years. During most of his reign, however, Zahir Shah's three uncles (and later his cousin) held actual power.

Soon after Zahir Shah took the throne, Afghanistan strengthened its ties with Western nations as well as reformist Islamic countries. In 1934 Afghanistan became a member of the League of Nations, an international organization of states that was a precursor to the United Nations. That same year, the United States established its first diplomatic mission in Afghanistan. In 1937 the country signed a mutual-defense treaty, the Saadabad Pact, with Iran, Iraq, and Turkey.

Foreign assistance was needed to help Afghanistan modernize, but because of the history of intense competition between Russia and Great Britain over the country, Zahir Shah and his advisers were reluctant to seek aid from either the British or the Soviets for fear of stirring up the rivals' mutual suspicion and antagonism. Instead, the rulers of Afghanistan invited teachers and experts from Germany to develop the country and its infrastructure.

Zahir Shah, shown here in a 1965 photo, was 19 years old when he became king of Afghanistan in 1933.

In spite of declaring itself neutral at the outbreak of World War II (1939–1945), Afghanistan hoped to survive in its traditional role of playing the British against the Russians. This time, however, Germany emerged as a third potential player in "the Great Game." The German threat could only be eliminated when Britain and Russia became allies—

after Hitler's attack on the Soviet Union in June 1941. The Allied powers were concerned about the sizeable community of German and Italian nationals, who at this time constituted by far the largest foreign presence in Afghanistan. The British and Soviets encouraged the king to expel these foreigners. Zahir Shah saw how the British and Soviets had occupied Iran in the summer of 1941 to prevent Germany from capturing the important oil fields in that country, and he acquiesced with the Allies' demands.

After the war Afghanistan seemed ready to continue its traditional role of **buffer state** between the great powers. In the immediate postwar years more Western influence was forthcoming. During the tenure of Zahir Shah's uncle Shah Mahmud as prime minister (1946–1953), Afghanistan cultivated good relations with the United States, which replaced Germany as the main financier of communications and irrigation projects. Afghanistan received aid from the United States, Western European countries, Japan, and the United Nations, which the government used for modernization in the areas of health, education, mining, and agriculture.

Shah Mahmud permitted open elections to the National Assembly and allowed opposition political groups to grow. Newspapers and student groups began calling for a more open political process. Shah Mahmud responded by shutting them down, but this brief period of movement toward a more open government would provide the seeds of revolution 30 years later.

The Pashtunistan Issue

The year 1947, when British India gained independence and was broken up into two sovereign countries, India and Pakistan, was also a turning point for Afghanistan. The new state of Pakistan, consisting of two halves separated by more than 1,000 miles (1,609 km) of Indian territory, contained in its western part—in Baluchistan and the North-West Frontier Province (NWFP)—members of the same tribes as lived in Afghanistan. Afghanistan demanded that the Pashtuns on the other side of the Durand Line be allowed a referendum to determine where and how they wanted to live, but the government of Pakistan, not wanting to give up territory to its neighbor, refused. Relations between the two countries grew tense, and the border passes were closed several times. The Afghan government openly encouraged the Pashtuns of the NWFP to establish an independent nation called Pashtunistan.

The Soviet Union was ready to support the idea of an independent Pashtunistan. This was a Cold War strategy, because formation of the new state would weaken Pakistan, an ally of the United States.

In 1953 Zahir Shah's cousin Muhammad Daoud, an advocate of Pashtunistan, replaced their uncle Shah Mahmud as prime minister. Daoud, though educated in the West, adopted a pro-Soviet orientation in foreign policy. In 1955, when the United States declined to fund Afghanistan's military, Daoud at once turned to Moscow for military assistance and training. A Soviet loan of about $100 million was secured for development projects, such as the construction of power plants and

Muhammad Daoud served as prime minister of Afghanistan from 1953 until 1963, when he was persuaded to resign because of the Pashtunistan dispute with Pakistan. Ten years later, Daoud deposed the king and seized power in a bloodless coup.

highways. Most important from the strategic point of view was the construction of military airfields and of the Salang Tunnel, enabling a country without railroads year-round passage across the Hindu Kush.

In 1961 Daoud tried to force the Pashtunistan issue by sending Afghan troops dressed as tribesmen across the Durand Line in an attempt to stir up a pro-Pashtunistan uprising. Pakistan responded by closing the border again, preventing landlocked Afghanistan from conducting trade with the Western world and forcing it to become more dependent on Soviet assistance. Afghanistan's economy suffered. In 1963, when it became clear that neither Daoud nor the president of Pakistan would give in, Zahir Shah asked Daoud to resign—which, surprisingly, he did.

The 1964 Constitution

Envisioning gradual movement toward democracy and modernization, Zahir Shah charged a commission of foreign-educated, non-royal Afghans to draft a new constitution. In 1964 a loya jirga (great tribal assembly) approved the constitution, which created a new legislature and included a bill of rights for all Afghans, including women. The lower house of Afghanistan's Parliament included legislators, many from rural districts, elected by the people.

But the constitution failed to specify many government functions and thus guaranteed that the king would maintain power. The cabinet acted on the king's wishes and held control over Parliament's upper house. As a result, relations between the cabinet and the lower house of Parliament weakened, and enthusiasm for the new constitution declined. Until 1973 the government hobbled along, barely able to make the constitution work.

In 1965 the Communist People's Democratic Party of Afghanistan (PDPA) won four seats in parliamentary elections. But Zahir Shah, fearful of the PDPA, refused to permit other new political parties, and the government grew more unstable. In 1973, while Zahir Shah was in Italy for medical treatment, Daoud seized power with a group of military officers. Zahir Shah's experiment with limited democracy had largely failed, and most Afghans welcomed Daoud's return. Royal rule in Afghanistan was over.

Communist Rule and the Soviet Invasion

Many saw Daoud as a forceful ruler who could bring order back to Afghanistan, even though he had aligned himself with the Communists. Daoud's PDPA allies in the military arrested hundreds of young members of the **Muslim Brotherhood**, an Islamic organization—founded in Egypt in the late 1920s— rejecting Western secularism and advocating that government and society be based on the tenets of the Qur'an. Many of the Muslim Brothers arrested in Afghanistan were executed. By 1975, however, Daoud had also dismissed the Communists from his cabinet, and in 1977 a loya jirga approved his new constitution, which created a presidential, one-party political system.

Although the Soviet Union continued to provide massive aid to Afghanistan during this time, relations between the two countries deteriorated as Daoud also sought aid agreements with India, Iran, and the oil-rich Arab states of Saudi Arabia, Iraq, and Kuwait. When economic conditions failed to improve despite foreign aid, Communist groups inside Afghanistan gained new followers. In 1978 Afghan Communists, allied with Afghan army and air force officers who had been trained in the Soviet Union, staged a bloody coup to overthrow Daoud, during which his entire family was massacred.

The PDPA called its takeover the Saur Revolution because it took place in the Islamic month of Saur. Under the leadership of Nur Muhammad Taraki, the PDPA implemented reforms, such as equal rights for women and changes in family law, which angered many traditionalists. They attempted a **land reform** program, in which tribal holdings of farmland were taken and

> The Soviet Union's ruthless, decade-long occupation of Afghanistan took an enormous toll in human suffering. About 1 million Afghans—many of them civilians—were killed, while an additional 5 million refugees fled to neighboring countries. The Soviet armed forces are believed to have suffered more than 30,000 dead.

redistributed among small farmers and farming cooperatives; this proved highly unpopular in Afghanistan, with its strong tribal history. The greatest losers, however, were members of Afghanistan's middle and upper classes, thousands of whom were killed and many more of whom were driven into exile.

Afghan exiles began organizing in Pakistan and Iran to resist the Communists, but the PDPA government also faced internal dissension between two polarized factions (Parcham and Khalq). Just months after the Saur Revolution, President Taraki was murdered by supporters of a rival leader, Hafizullah Amin. Although the Soviet leadership had supported Taraki and was suspicious of Amin, the coup had occurred too suddenly for Moscow to intervene.

Amin was known as a rigid Communist, but once in power he tried to win the support of Afghan Muslim leaders by discontinuing some of the state's anti-religious policies. However, these measures did little to erase hostility among the population or to decrease the state of high alarm in Moscow. The Soviets feared that Amin's government might further antagonize the Muslim population and that Islamists might overthrow the government and establish an Islamic **theocracy**, as had occurred in neighboring Iran during late 1978 and early 1979 under the leadership of the Ayatollah Khomeini.

In the last days of December 1979, the Soviets invaded Afghanistan, intending to overthrow Amin. Soviet troops captured Kabul, assassinated

Amin, and installed Babrak Karmal in his place. However, resistance to Soviet troops grew quickly and fiercely. Resistance leaders appealed to all Afghans on the basis of their Muslim identity and tribal nationalism. The fighters who resisted became known as mujahedin, which means "those waging jihad." The word *jihad* literally means "struggle" and refers to Muslims' resistance to any kind of obstacle to their faith. For the mujahedin, this meant actual warfare in resisting the Soviet invaders, whom they saw as "godless" and repressive of their religion. Many of the leaders of the resistance had been university students in the 1970s, when they had organized with groups like the Muslim Brotherhood against the growing Communist presence in their country.

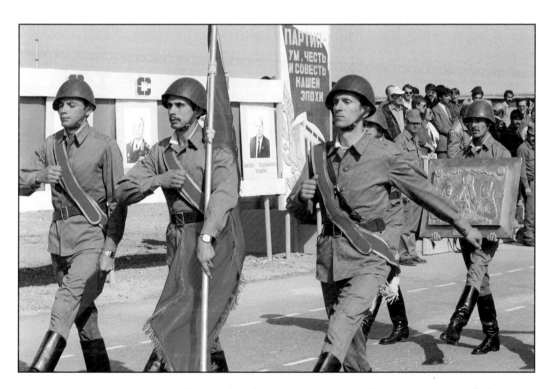

Soviet troops march through downtown Kabul, 1986. Instability in Afghanistan, and concerns that the ideology of the Islamic Revolution might spread from neighboring Iran, led the Soviet Union to invade Afghanistan in late 1979 in order to prop up a pro-Communist government.

For most of 1979, while the chaos in Afghanistan was brewing, the United States remained focused on neighboring Iran. Khomeini's Islamic Revolution had toppled a government that had been a strategic U.S. ally in the Cold War. Both the United States and the Soviet Union felt threatened by the Islamic Revolution, and Moscow had ordered the invasion of Afghanistan as a preventive measure to keep the revolution from spreading into Central Asia. From the U.S. point of view, however, the U.S.S.R.'s offensive move looked like an attempt to change the fragile balance of power in Southwest Asia; therefore the United States would try to thwart and contain the Soviets' efforts. Under President Jimmy Carter, but especially during the administration of his successor, Ronald Reagan, the United States funneled aid to Afghans resisting the Soviet occupation. In the Reagan years, financial aid was given to Pakistan, which in turn passed money and weapons to the mujahedin, who trained at secret bases in Peshawar and elsewhere. Money for arms also flowed in from China, Egypt, and Saudi Arabia, while international aid arrived in Pakistan for the more than 3 million Afghan refugees there. Muslim nations denounced the Soviet invasion, and the United Nations passed numerous resolutions condemning the occupation. Through the U.N., Pakistan and Afghanistan began peace talks in 1982 and were later joined by the Soviet Union and United States.

The Soviet-sponsored government in Kabul tried to build popular support for its initiatives. For example, it called a loya jirga in 1985 to ratify the country's new constitution. It tried to control the Pashtun tribe and sought good relations with the country's minority tribes (Uzbek, Turkman, and Tajik) by supporting their cultural traditions. The government also reached out to the refugees in and around Kabul, giving them food and fuel if they agreed to join the PDPA.

But the resistance grew further. Mujahedin groups within Afghanistan had increasing success ambushing Soviet troops in the rugged countryside, and U.S.-supplied, shoulder-fired Stinger missiles took a heavy toll on Soviet aircraft. The Soviets responded brutally, targeting especially the rural Afghan population, even noncombatants; in many instances entire villages were annihilated. As the casualties on both sides mounted, Karmal resigned and was succeeded by another Communist, Muhammad Najibullah. Although Najibullah promised to respect Islam, the mujahedin rebuffed his offers of a settlement.

By the mid-1980s the Afghan occupation had become highly costly for, and highly unpopular in, the Soviet Union. When a new Soviet leader, Mikhail Gorbachev, came to power in 1985 with plans to restructure and reform the U.S.S.R's economy and political system, he recognized that success in those endeavors would require that the Soviet Union extricate itself from the quagmire in Afghanistan.

In April 1988 the governments of Pakistan and Afghanistan—with the Soviet Union and the United States acting as guarantors—reached an agreement to settle the Afghan conflict. Under the terms of the agreement, the Soviet Union would withdraw its troops, refugees would be permitted to return home without fear of persecution, and Afghanistan would be a neutral state. The mujahedin accepted the agreement, and by February 1989 all Soviet troops had left the country.

Civil War and the Rise of the Taliban

Afghanistan had been devastated by a decade of Soviet occupation and fierce fighting. As many as 1 million Afghans had lost their lives as a result of the conflict. An estimated 5 million Afghan refugees had fled to Pakistan or Iran. Afghanistan's economy was shattered, its infrastructure in ruins. Unexploded land mines littered much of the countryside.

After the conflict had been settled, plans were made for a transitional government and a new constitution. But the mujahedin refused to cooperate and began to attack Najibullah's forces. Najibullah declared a national emergency and the Soviet Union sent in huge shipments of military and economic aid. With this help, the army was able to beat back mujahedin attacks on the cities for a while. However, in 1992 an alliance of mujahedin captured Kabul and set up the Islamic State of Afghanistan, with Burhanuddin Rabbani as interim president.

But the various mujahedin groups failed to devise a political system that combined their more traditional tribal system with modern political concepts. They continued to fight—though now not against Soviet occupiers or a Communist regime in Kabul, but against one another. Afghanistan was split into small territories held by rival mujahedin factions, usually dominated by a local warlord. Rival warlords profited from drug trafficking and were accused of extortion, kidnapping, burglary, and rampant violence against women.

This corruption and unrest paved the way for a new regime, the Taliban, to gain power. A *talib* is a Muslim religious student, and most members of the group that in the early 1990s became known as the Taliban were educated in religious schools, called *madrassas*, set up for Afghan boys in Pakistan. Madrassas had been part of the Muslim educational system for a millennium, but several factors affected the education young Afghans received in the madrassas in Pakistan. First, schools in the Pakistan refugee camps were run in the Deobandi tradition. This is a movement within Islam that had originated among Muslims in British India, with the goal of ridding the religion of all foreign influences. Second, the madrassas in Pakistan were operated largely by mullahs who were poorly educated in Islamic law and history. And most of these madrassas were funded by Muslim foundations based in Saudi Arabia, which ensured that the strict branch of Islam dominant in that country, known as **Wahhabism**, would have a great influence on the students.

During the 1980s the Afghan talibs were involved in combat against Soviet forces. For the most part they were Pashtuns under the command of largely Pashtun resistance groups. But the Taliban movement later emerged in Afghanistan as a unified military force, capitalizing on broad dissatisfaction with the local warlords in the Kandahar area. Under the leadership of Mullah Muhammad Omar, the Taliban vowed to create a "pure" Islamic state and govern Afghanistan using a strict interpretation of Sharia. In late 1994 Pakistan chose a group of well-trained Taliban soldiers to protect the road convoy system that ran across Afghanistan and connected Pakistan with Central Asia. This group successfully fought off warlords and rival mujahedin groups and then took control of Kandahar. In 1996 the Taliban occupied Jalalabad and Kabul. By mid-1997 the Taliban controlled two-thirds of the country.

Under Omar's leadership, the Taliban were initially quite popular with the Afghan people, weary from years of chaos and abuses at the hands of

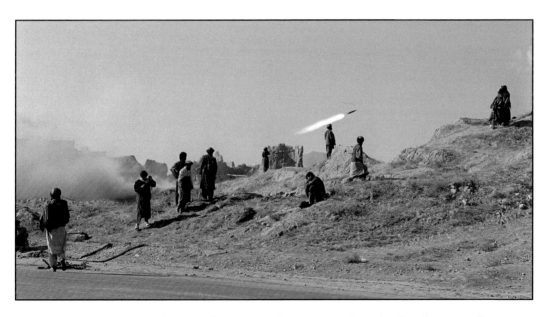

Members of the Taliban militia watch as a rocket is fired toward enemy positions during a 1996 battle outside Kabul. After the Soviets withdrew in 1989, Afghanistan descended into civil war. Mujahedin factions that had united to resist the foreign invasion turned on each other in a struggle for control of the country, ultimately paving the way for the Taliban.

the warlords. The Taliban had notable success in restoring order in the country and opening the roads. They stressed their devotion as Muslims and, as promised, strictly enforced Sharia. They banned computers, movies, televisions, and radios, claiming these exerted an anti-Islamic influence. They also banned music, photography, paintings, sculpture, and any picture of humans or animals. They established laws requiring men to wear beards at least a fist-length below the chin. Improper beard lengths might result in a public beating, while theft could result in amputation of a limb and those arrested for murder were executed.

But the Taliban's most stringent laws affected women and girls. Girls were banned from schools, and women could no longer hold jobs, which caused an employment crisis in education and health care. In public, women were also required to wear the *burqa*, a garment that covers the entire body, with only a crocheted section over the eyes through which to see. Designed to enforce the custom of secluding women from men, the burqa had long been worn by some women in Afghanistan, but the Taliban made it a requirement for all women. Those caught not wearing one were subject to extreme punishment. Women caught outside their home without a male relative could be beaten or shot. A woman caught wearing fingernail polish could have her fingertips chopped off. Executions and punishments such as flogging took place publicly in Afghan soccer stadiums.

In spite of the international outcry, the Taliban also destroyed important pieces of Afghanistan's cultural heritage. These included artifacts from the National Museum in Kabul, historical sites in Ghazni, and a pair of enormous ancient statues of Buddha in Bamiyan Province.

Only Pakistan, Saudi Arabia, and the United Arab Emirates officially recognized the Taliban government. (Iran—which, like Afghanistan, was an Islamic theocracy—did not recognize the Taliban largely for sectarian reasons: the Taliban followed the Sunni branch of Islam, Iran the Shia branch.)

The Taliban regime imposed a harsh interpretation of Islamic law. For example, women were not permitted to work, attend school, or go out in public unless fully covered (the women here are wearing a garment called a burqa) and accompanied by a male relative. Those who violated these rules were beaten or sometimes even killed.

The Taliban's status as an international pariah was solidified by its policy of permitting terrorist organizations to operate training camps in Afghanistan. Among these groups was al-Qaeda, an international Islamist terrorist network that seeks to rid the Muslim world of what it regards as the destructive influence of the West and to replace secular governments with *fundamentalist* Islamic regimes. Al-Qaeda's founder, a wealthy Saudi named Osama bin Laden, had first gone to Afghanistan during the 1980s, to join the mujahedin in their fight against the Soviet occupation. In that effort he probably received aid, at least indirectly, from both Saudi Arabia and the United States. But by the early 1990s bin Laden had become a fierce opponent of the Saudi monarchy and the United States. Five years after fleeing Saudi Arabia in 1991, he settled in Afghanistan, where the Taliban provided him sanctuary and he supported the Taliban financially. In 1996 bin Laden issued a "declaration of jihad" whose stated goals included overthrowing the Saudi monarchy and driving out all U.S. troops stationed on the Arabian Peninsula. Two years later he called on all devout Muslims to kill Americans anywhere in the world. Al-Qaeda was implicated in several terrorist attacks against U.S. targets, including the August 8, 1998, bombings of the American embassies in Kenya and Tanzania, which together killed more than 220 people and injured nearly 4,600. In 1999 and 2000, the United Nations Security Council passed resolutions demanding that the Taliban close all terrorist training camps in Afghanistan and hand over bin Laden for trial, but the Taliban refused.

While the Taliban controlled most of Afghanistan, a coalition of diverse opposition groups, officially led by the deposed president Burhanuddin Rabbani and called the Northern Alliance, held substantial pieces of territory in the north. In contrast with the Taliban, which was composed largely of members of the Pashtun tribe, the Northern Alliance represented Afghanistan's minority tribes—the Tajiks, Hazara, Uzbeks, and Turkmen. On September 9, 2001, Taliban soldiers assassinated the Northern Alliance's powerful military commander, Ahmed Shah Masood, and, with the exception of several small pockets, gained control of the north.

After September 11

Two days after the killing of Ahmed Shah Masood, terrorists hijacked four American jetliners and carried out the suicide attacks on the World Trade Center in New York City and the Pentagon outside Washington, D.C. (One of the planes, also believed to be headed for Washington, crashed in a field in western Pennsylvania.) Blame for the attacks quickly fell on Osama bin Laden's al-Qaeda organization, and U.S. president

George W. Bush demanded that the Taliban turn over bin Laden. The Taliban refused.

On October 7 the United States and the United Kingdom began a war to topple the Taliban regime and capture or kill the al-Qaeda terrorists who were being sheltered in Afghanistan. The size of the U.S. and British forces deployed in the campaign was relatively small; most of the ground fighting was done by the Northern Alliance, with material and logistical help, along with crucial air support, from the United States. After a six-week bombing campaign, Northern Alliance fighters advanced rapidly. By late November, Kabul had been taken, and by early December the rout of the Taliban was complete.

Even before the fighting had ended, representatives of the major Afghan opposition and exile groups convened in Bonn, Germany, under the auspices of the United Nations to discuss the future of Afghanistan. One of the most pressing concerns was the establishment of an interim administration to govern the country before elections could be held. Particularly contentious was the question of who should lead that interim government. Though some hoped the former king Zahir Shah might return to lead Afghanistan, the Bonn Conference selected Hamid Karzai, who had fought with the mujahedin against the Soviets, to preside over the interim government. Karzai's father had been a member of the Afghan Parliament in the 1970s and the head of a powerful Pashtun clan with long ties to the monarchy. A loya jirga assembled the following June and elected Karzai president of the Transitional Islamic State of Afghanistan (TISA). Another loya jirga approved a new Afghan constitution in January 2004.

National elections to choose the president of a permanent government—originally slated for June 2004 but postponed because of security concerns—were finally held in October of that year. Hamid Karzai won decisively, with more than 55 percent of the vote; his nearest rival claimed just 16 percent. Although several of Karzai's opponents initially indicated that they might not accept the outcome of the election, claiming widespread fraud, they eventually conceded. While independent election observers acknowledged that some fraud had indeed occurred, they believed that it was not nearly extensive enough to have made a difference in the results.

The relatively smooth elections, large turnout (more than 8 million Afghan voters, including women, had voted, despite lingering threats of violence), and Karzai's clear mandate were encouraging signs that Afghanistan had entered on a path to political stability and democracy after decades of strife. And in 2005, legislative elections were held and the National Assembly held its first meeting.

Yet optimism was tempered by the sheer magnitude of the problems confronting Afghanistan. Even after his landslide electoral victory, President Karzai's national government exercised only limited control outside the capital city—though the situation was no longer as bad as it had been through 2003, when Karzai had been referred to sarcastically as "the mayor of Kabul." Nevertheless, the Taliban had reemerged as a dangerous force, particularly in the south-central region around Kandahar. Taliban attacks slowed reconstruction efforts and convinced some international aid agencies to pull their workers out of Afghanistan. Al-Qaeda remnants continued to find safe haven along the Afghanistan-Pakistan border (the old Durand Line) despite the presence of U.S. forces tasked with hunting for bin Laden, Mullah Muhammad Omar, and other al-Qaeda and Taliban leaders. Even more problematic, warlords commanding large, often heavily armed militias (some estimates put the total number of militia members as high as 500,000) were in control of several provinces. Analysts believed that Karzai would either have to find ways to co-opt the warlords or, more likely, to disarm them; yet it was not certain that the new Afghan National Army (ANA) was up to such a task.

Since President Karzai was sworn into office in December 2004, Afghanistan has confronted serious economic issues. Despite billions of dollars of humanitarian and reconstruction aid from the United States and other donors, Afghanistan remains a land of crushing poverty. Sanitation facilities and safe drinking water are largely lacking, health care is scarce, and the education system is in shambles. Already the dominant producer, Afghanistan produced a record opium poppy crop in 2007, supplying 93 percent of the world's opium.

National election workers wade through bundles of presidential ballots at a counting center in Kabul, October 2004. More than 8 million Afghans voted in the October 9 presidential election, with Hamid Karzai receiving the support of upwards of 55 percent. Although some of the contenders for the presidency initially claimed that the election had been rigged in Karzai's favor, international observers declared the voting to have been for the most part free and fair.

Former Afghan king Zahir Shah gestures during the opening ceremony of the loya jirga in Kabul, June 2002. After the overthrow of the Taliban government, the former king played a symbolic role in Afghanistan's transition to democracy.

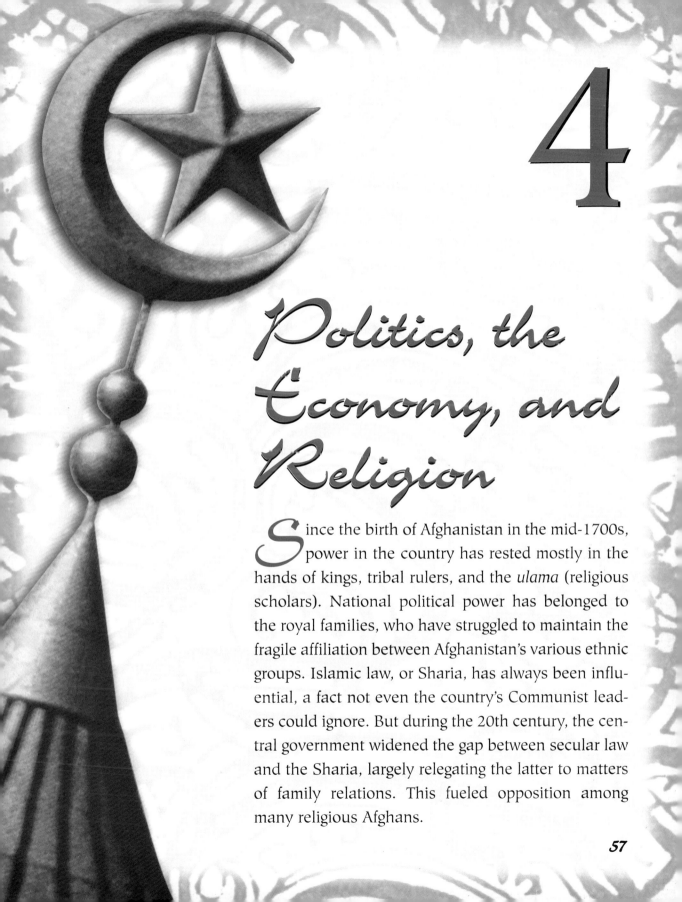

Politics, the Economy, and Religion

S ince the birth of Afghanistan in the mid-1700s, power in the country has rested mostly in the hands of kings, tribal rulers, and the *ulama* (religious scholars). National political power has belonged to the royal families, who have struggled to maintain the fragile affiliation between Afghanistan's various ethnic groups. Islamic law, or Sharia, has always been influential, a fact not even the country's Communist leaders could ignore. But during the 20th century, the central government widened the gap between secular law and the Sharia, largely relegating the latter to matters of family relations. This fueled opposition among many religious Afghans.

Today, as Afghanistan attempts to emerge from a quarter century of war, the country faces a double challenge: how to transform its central government into a representative democracy while maintaining national allegiance to Islam. Its experiment in combining Western-style democracy with Islamic principles is being watched closely around the world.

But the main obstacle to Afghanistan's progress remains its devastated economy. In the short term, only international aid and massive reconstruction will provide the stability needed to institute fundamental political reforms.

Politics in Afghanistan

Though some scholars believe the tradition of the assembly of tribal elders, the loya jirga, extends back as much as 1,000 years, it became a staple of Afghan politics in 1747, when a loya jirga of Pashtun representatives appointed Ahmad Shah as the leader of Afghanistan. There are two types of loya jirga. The first, called by Afghan citizens at any time of national crisis, decides such matters as going to war or electing a king. The second is called by the nation's leaders to consult on matters such as new laws and international treaties. Loya jirga members have traditionally included royalty, government officials, and tribal, regional, religious, political, and military leaders.

The king and the king's family dominated the government of Afghanistan from the time Ahmad Shah was appointed king until the 1960s. The country's first constitutions, passed in 1923 and 1931, promised a **constitutional monarchy**, though the government more closely resembled a royal **oligarchy**. The 1931 constitution did incorporate Islamic judges into the judiciary, but it also established a national secular body of law. In the late 1940s the prime minister briefly experimented with increased political freedom, but that period of liberalization was short-lived.

It wasn't until 1963 that the first non-royal was appointed prime minister. The following year, a loya jirga adopted a new constitution that instituted a constitutional monarchy based on the separation of executive, legislative, and judicial branches. Though the constitution left significant power in the hands of the king, it stipulated that no member of the royal family other than the king could participate in government. The constitution also stressed individual over tribal rights and secular over religious principles. While declaring that no law contrary to Islam could be passed, the constitution also specified that all laws would be passed by Parliament and signed by the king and that Islamic law would be used only when no relevant national law existed.

In 1973 Muhammad Daoud staged a coup and took control from King Zahir Shah, his cousin, ending royal rule. The constitution he had approved in 1977 created a presidential, one-party political system. After the Soviet invasion in 1979, the Soviet-backed Communist government continued the presidential, one-party system and tried to institute wide-ranging social reforms, which merely increased opposition to Communist rule.

Following the overthrow of the Communist government by the mujahedin in April 1992, an interim council took control. But regional fragmentation and warlordism, rather than the development of a strong central authority, ensued. The disorder paved the way for the Taliban, which, once in power, ignored all previous government institutions, establishing a theocracy and enforcing a draconian version of the Sharia with extreme public punishments.

The Transitional Islamic State of Afghanistan

After the Northern Alliance—aided by the United States, Britain, and other members of the anti-Taliban coalition—ended Taliban rule in 2001, the U.N. convened a meeting of delegates from Afghanistan's major ethnic, religious, and political groups (not including the Taliban) in Bonn, Germany, to formulate a new government. With strong international support, the Bonn Agreement established a temporary government known as the Afghan Interim Authority (AIA). Headed by Hamid Karzai, it featured a 30-member cabinet that represented all of Afghanistan's ethnic groups and included two women. The agreement called for a commission to write a new constitution and another to establish a new Afghan justice system based on international legal standards, the rule of law, Islamic principles, and Afghan legal traditions. It also specified that a transitional government should be in place within six months.

In April 2002 Zahir Shah, the former king, returned to Afghanistan but declared he would make no claim to the throne. In June of that year, a 1,050-member loya jirga composed of a diverse cross-section of Afghan society—including elected representatives, religious leaders, government officials, women, internally displaced people, refugees, and nomads—convened to create a new parliament. The loya jirga elected Hamid Karzai president of the Transitional Islamic State of Afghanistan (TISA). According to the terms of the Bonn Agreement, the TISA was then to hold a loya jirga within 18 months to adopt a constitution and, within 24 months, to hold nationwide elections for a permanent government.

The New Constitution

A special commission began drafting a new constitution, based on the 1964 constitution and on public opinion gathered from a cross-section of Afghan citizens and Afghan refugees in neighboring Pakistan and Iran. In early January 2004, the constitution was approved by a constitutional loya jirga, which included 502 members, most of them elected representatives.

The new constitution calls for a democratic form of government similar in many respects to that of the United States. It specifies a strong

A United Nations official watches as a delegate casts his vote for Afghanistan's transitional leader during a session of the 2002 loya jirga. Hamid Karzai won election for a 24-month term as Afghanistan's interim president.

central government with separation of powers between the executive, legislative, and judicial branches.

The executive branch, elected by popular vote, includes a president and two vice presidents. They serve for five-year terms and are limited to two consecutive terms.

The legislative branch comprises the two-chamber National Assembly, made up of the lower House of People (*Wolesi Jirga*) and the upper House of Elders (*Meshrano Jirga*). Members of the House of People are elected by popular vote to five-year terms; provinces are allocated representatives in proportion to their population. In an effort to encourage women's participation, the constitution specifies that at least 25 percent of the seats in the

House of People be set aside for women. The House of Elders, the National Assembly's upper chamber, consists of elected and appointed members whose terms run for five, four, or three years. The president appoints one-third of the body's members, and half of those appointed must be women.

With the country's past in mind, the new constitution also abides by human rights standards as defined by the U.N. and international agreements. For example, the constitution declares women the equal of men under Afghan law and says the government must promote women's equality through education and other means. It also requires the government to keep track of human rights abuses through an independent commission.

Zahir Shah looks on as Hamid Karzai signs Afghanistan's constitution during a ceremony in January 2004. The new constitution created a democratic government with executive, legislative, and judicial branches.

However, the constitution does institute a kind of "theocratic democracy" by declaring Islam the official religion of the nation and forbidding any law "contrary to the beliefs and provisions of the sacred religion of Islam." The independent court system established by the constitution—consisting of a supreme court, high courts, and appeals courts—has the power of judicial review of legislation and acts of government. This was not the case with earlier Afghan courts, and it may mean that the nation's judges will play a crucial role in settling legal conflicts between secular and religious principles.

Critics of the new constitution argue that it gives too much control to the president—who, in addition to appointing one-third of the House of Elders, appoints top judges and national security officials. Supporters of the constitution respond by saying that, like the U.S. government, the new Afghan government will have enough checks and balances to ensure a sharing of power. For example, the constitution gives the National Assembly veto power over key presidential appointments and policies, and a special commission is supposed to monitor implementation of the constitution.

The constitutional loya jirga was plagued by disagreements between ethnic groups. In particular, the Pashtun supporters of Karzai's government struggled with Tajiks and Uzbeks over the issue of language. In the end, the constitution declared Pashtu (spoken by Pashtuns) and Dari (a variant of Persian spoken by many other Afghans) the country's two official languages and gave northern minority languages official status in their geographic areas.

Political Parties

Power in Afghanistan has traditionally resided in the tribe and village; political parties did not exist in Afghanistan until the 1960s. After the Communists took over the government in 1978, dozens of political groups emerged, but later the Taliban suppressed all political parties. In 2003 President Karzai approved a law allowing political parties to organize, citing the freedom to form political parties as necessary to the development of a multi-party democracy. Since then, political parties have organized at a rapid pace. Among the many groups forming their own parties have been Islamic leaders, mujahedin, Taliban, former Communist Party members, Afghan refugees, and tribal elders.

The Economy

Even before the Soviet Union invaded in 1979, Afghanistan was one of the world's poorest countries. The Soviet occupation, subsequent civil conflict, and Taliban rule led to further economic deterioration. Today Afghanistan depends heavily on foreign aid, but its economy is growing. Growth from 2003 to 2007 averaged about 15 percent per year.

Afghan leaders first began seriously pursuing economic development in the 1930s, founding banks, introducing paper money, and expanding the education system. In the 1950s the government began to improve irrigation, roads, telecommunications, and manufacturing. The country also established better international trade relationships and received foreign aid for infrastructure projects such as roads, dams, airports, factories, and irrigation. By the late 1970s, however, the economy was declining because of a lack of money and a shortage of skilled workers.

After the Soviet invasion, Western nations cut off economic aid, and Afghanistan became economically dependent on the Soviet Union. Economic conditions remained bleak under the Taliban regime. Also, from 1979 to the end of Taliban rule, approximately one-third of all Afghans fled to Pakistan or Iran, removing money for investment and decimating the country's labor force. And war destroyed many of the country's roads, irrigation systems, and industrial facilities, hindering normal economic activity. As a result, the ***gross domestic product***

(GDP) fell dramatically. Severe droughts from 1998–2002 and again in 2006 compounded the problem. Isolated northern provinces were hit especially hard by both drought and heavy fighting.

International Aid

At the Tokyo Donors Conference for Afghan Reconstruction in early 2002, more than 60 countries and financial institutions pledged $4.5 billion in aid through 2006. Not all of the aid packages were actually delivered, however. At a second donors conference in Bonn, Germany, in March 2004, more than 50 countries pledged an additional $8.2 billion in aid for the next three years. But, as humanitarian organizations point out, per capita aid for Afghans is significantly lower than that for other nations with similar levels of need.

Decades of war devastated Afghanistan's economy and its infrastructure; since the overthrow of the Taliban, foreign aid has been used to rebuild buildings, bridges, aqueducts, and other facilities. These Afghan workers are building a road.

Afghanistan's poverty rate is difficult to ascertain, but 2003 estimates range to more than 50 percent. Infant mortality is among the highest in the world, as is illiteracy. Hamid Karzai has pledged to transform Afghanistan into a self-sustaining country, but due to these and other problems, international aid is likely to be crucial for the foreseeable future.

Economic Sectors and Development

The main source of income in Afghanistan remains agriculture, in spite of the fact that only 12 percent of the country's land is arable and less than 10 percent is actually farmed. Most Afghans still eke out a living from their rugged land in ways developed centuries ago, providing for their families by farming and raising livestock.

Major crops include wheat, rice, barley, corn, vegetables, fruits, and nuts. Sheep raising is also important; major sheep products include wool and the valuable skins of the Karakul (Persian lamb) breed.

Afghan nomads, who make up as much as 10 percent of the population, tend mostly Karakul but also have goats, cattle, donkeys, and horses in their flocks. The nomads sell animals, wool, skins, and dairy products to farmers and merchants.

Farmers rely on winter snows and spring rains for their water supply, but many of their irrigation systems were destroyed during fighting in the countryside. Land mines scattered across the country have also caused many to reduce the size of their crops or stop farming altogether. A four-year drought starting in 1999 also decreased agricultural production dramatically, but in 2003 adequate rainfall led to the largest wheat harvest since before the invasion by the Soviet Union. Nevertheless, millions of Afghans, especially those in rural areas, continue to rely on international food aid. At a cost of $378 million, the United Nations World Food Programme distributed 550,000 metric tons of food aid to over 7 million Afghans by December 2008.

Industry plays a comparatively minor role in Afghanistan's economy.

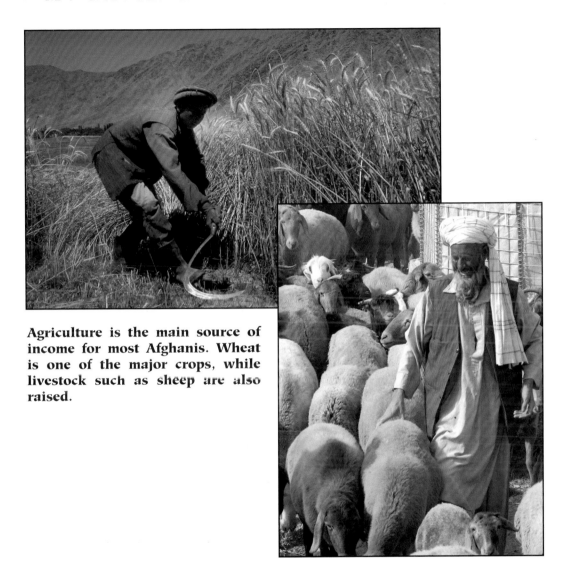

Agriculture is the main source of income for most Afghanis. Wheat is one of the major crops, while livestock such as sheep are also raised.

Goods such as textiles, leather, soap, furniture, shoes, cement, fertilizer, and processed foods are produced on a small scale. Handicrafts may constitute Afghanistan's main industry. Particularly important are handwoven rugs, which are produced mostly by families working at home.

Afghanistan has modest mineral resources, including natural gas and some oil reserves, though these deposits have yet to be fully exploited. Afghans have long engaged in the small-scale mining of gems, gold, copper,

The Economy of Afghanistan

Gross domestic product (GDP)*: $35 billion

GDP per capita: $1,000

Inflation: 13%

Natural resources: natural gas, petroleum, coal, copper, chromite, talc, barites, sulfur, lead, zinc, iron ore, salt, precious and semiprecious stones

Agriculture (38% of GDP): opium, wheat, fruits, nuts, wool, mutton, sheepskins, lambskins (2005 est.)

Industry (24% of GDP): small-scale production of textiles, soap, furniture, shoes, fertilizer, cement; handwoven carpets; natural gas, coal, copper (2005 est.)

Services (38% of GDP): government services (including education, health care, and the military), small enterprises (2005 est.)

Foreign trade:

  Imports—$3.823 billion: capital goods, food, textiles, petroleum products (2006 est.)

  Exports—$274 million (not including illicit exports): opium, fruits and nuts, handwoven carpets, wool, cotton, hides and pelts, precious and semiprecious gems (2006 est.)

Currency exchange rate: 50.51 Afghanistan afghanis = U.S. $1 (September 2008)

*Gross domestic product (GDP) is the total value of goods and services produced annually (here estimated using the purchasing power parity method).

All figures are 2003 estimates unless otherwise noted.

Sources: CIA World Factbook, 2008; Bloomberg.com.

and coal. The Soviets exported natural gas by pipeline into the Soviet Union in the 1980s, but by the mid-1990s, little mineral or oil and gas extraction was occurring because of damaged infrastructure, limited trade relationships with other countries, and ongoing conflict in the countryside. Soviet geologists identified more than a dozen natural gas and oil fields in the northern part of Afghanistan, which were capped following the withdrawal of Soviet troops in 1989. The country's instability and the demise of trade with the former Soviet Union have delayed the expansion and reopening of the gas lines. Mining attempts also remain problematic.

Trade accounts for only a small portion of the Afghan economy, but imports and exports have been increasing since the fall of the Taliban. Afghanistan's chief trading partners include Pakistan and India, and trade relationships are forming with Central Asian countries. Afghanistan's chief exports (excluding smuggled and illegal exports) are carpets and agricultural products. Afghanistan's governments, including the Taliban, once benefited enormously from the smuggling of goods into Pakistan, but recent efforts to reduce this activity have had some success.

One especially pressing problem facing the government is how to stop the illegal production and smuggling of opium (from which heroin is derived). Afghanistan produces 93 percent of the world's opium, and the illicit opium and heroin trade hit an all-time high in 2003, accounting for more than half of the country's GDP by some estimates. A hint of the difficulty the government will have in curtailing this problem can be gleaned from statistics reported by the United Nations Office on Drugs and Crime (UNODC). In 2003, the UNODC said, the average income per hectare (2.47 acres) of opium poppy grown in Afghanistan was $12,700, compared with just $222 per acre of wheat. That is not to say that all or most of the farmers cultivating opium were rich, as much of the total poppy crop was grown on large landholdings. Yet according to the UNODC, the average net income of a farmer who cultivated poppy (along with other crops) stood at $2,520 in 2003, while non-poppy farmers averaged just $670. In a country as poor as Afghanistan, growing opium poppy, though illegal, is a highly attractive option. Thus, government attempts to combat the problem must

A group of men harvest juice from the bulbs of poppy plants; this juice is used to make the drug opium, which in turn can be processed into an even stronger narcotic, heroin. Afghanistan is the world's largest producer of opium.

focus not simply on law enforcement and crop eradication but also on providing economically viable alternatives to poppy cultivation. The task has assumed increased importance because a large portion of the enormous profits generated by the illegal drug trade are believed to go to Afghan warlords, and even to terrorists. President Karzai continues to seek aid from donor countries as part of a five-year plan to reduce opium cultivation 70 percent by 2008. Afghanistan has also signed an agreement with its six neighboring countries to work together to fight the illegal drug trade. In the second half of 2008, the UNODC reported a 19 percent decrease in opium cultivation to 157,000 hectares, compared to the record harvest of 193,000 in 2007. According to the UNODC report, the number of opium-free provinces has increased by almost 50 percent since 2007. Still, the UNODC estimated that cleared regions composed less than 10 percent of the area under poppy cultivation.

Another major obstacle to economic development in Afghanistan is environmental devastation caused by the combination of recent wars, poverty, and drought. Rivers have run dry, orchards have been stripped, hillside farms have eroded, and livestock have extensively overgrazed pastures. Poor irrigation practices have also added salt to the soil, reducing or even destroying its fertility.

Religion in Afghanistan

Approximately 99 percent of Afghans are Muslim. The remaining 1 percent includes Hindus, Sikhs, and Zoroastrians. Virtually all Jews who had been living in Afghanistan immigrated to Israel or the United States by the mid-1980s.

Zoroastrianism flourished in what is now Afghanistan from the fifth century B.C.E. until the Greeks invaded the region in the fourth century C.E. The Mauryan (Indian) dynasty later brought Buddhism to the region. But Islam arrived in the region in 637 C.E., just five years after the death of the prophet Muhammad, and overcame all these religious influences to become the dominant religion in Afghanistan by the ninth century.

The Sunni-Shia Split

After Muhammad's death in 632 C.E., Muslim leaders chose his close companion Abu Bakr, the father of Muhammad's youngest wife, to be his successor as head of the Muslim community (caliph). Others, however, believed leadership should remain in Muhammad's family, and thus his successor should be Ali, the Prophet's cousin and son-in-law. (Muhammad had no sons who survived to adulthood.) Ali eventually did become caliph, in 656, but he was assassinated several years later. In 680 Ali's son Hussein asserted his claim to the caliphate, leading to a civil war with the powerful Umayyads, who would establish the first Islamic dynasty. At the Battle of Karbala, in present-day Iraq, the Umayyad forces

Nearly all Afghans follow Islam, a monotheistic religion that was established in the seventh century by the prophet Muhammad. These Afghan Muslims are participating in a prayer service outside the Id Gah Mosque in Kabul.

slaughtered Hussein, his small army, and many members of his family. After this, Muslims who supported the line of succession from Ali, called the Shia, split permanently from the larger branch of Sunni Islam.

Though the Sunni-Shia schism originally developed as a disagreement over leadership, it has over the centuries come to encompass all matters of belief and law. Today, Sunnis constitute the vast majority of the world's Muslims—an estimated 85 percent. In Afghanistan, Sunnis outnumber Shiites by about four to one.

The Shia branch of Islam is further divided into the Imami (the Twelvers) and the Ismaili (the Seveners) sects, both of which are represented in Afghanistan. The Imamis recognize 12 successive Imams (infallible, divinely appointed leaders in the line of Ali), while the Ismailis rejected the heir designated by the sixth Imam, whom the Imamis accepted. Ismailis are secretive about their unique beliefs, and the Imamis do not consider Ismailis true Muslims. Many Afghans are suspicious of the Ismailis in their midst, and Ismailis are often very poor.

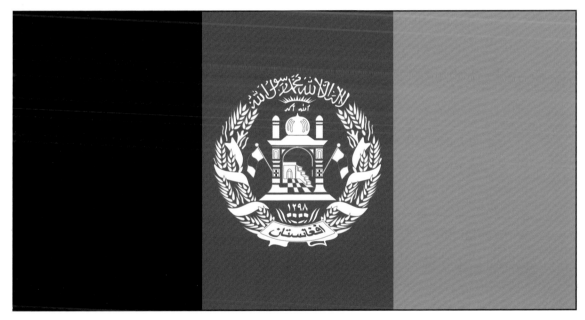

Afghanistan's new flag, first flown in early 2002, and altered slightly in 2004, closely resembles the monarchy flag of 1930–1974, which was banned by the Soviets. The flag includes equal vertical bands of green, red, and black. In the middle is a white insignia composed of a *mehrab*, the niche in a mosque wall that indicates the direction of Mecca, and a *menber*, a many-tiered pulpit. The insignia is flanked by two flags and ensconced in sheaves of wheat, and above it is written the Islamic profession of faith, "There is no God but Allah and Muhammad is his prophet."

Sunni, Imami, and Ismaili groups tend to remain segregated throughout Afghanistan, though they do mix in certain areas, such as Bamiyan Province. During the political negotiations between rival mujahedin groups leading up to the formation of the Islamic State of Afghanistan in 1992, Shia groups attempted to gain more rights, but were unsuccessful. Some Sunni groups responded with violence, and serious confrontations took place, especially in and around Kabul.

The rise of the powerful Sunni Ghaznavid dynasty in the 10th century prevented the spread of Shiism from Iran into Afghanistan, keeping the area west of Iran into South Asia predominantly Sunni. And Sunni Islam proved very resilient in Afghanistan. Even Genghis Khan's brutal and sweeping Mongol invasion of the early 1200s, which destroyed Islamic institutions and decimated the population, could not uproot it. Within 100 years, Genghis Khan's successors had themselves converted to Islam.

Sufism

Sufism, the **mystical** tradition within Islam, is an important element in both the Sunni and Shia communities in Afghanistan. Its influence is seen in both rural and urban settings, but especially among the middle classes. Sufi practice first developed in the eighth century among Muslims unhappy with what they regarded as an overemphasis on the law in Islam. Sufis attempt to draw near to God through meditation, song, music, and ecstatic dance.

The Herat area has the largest variety of Sufi branches, which are headed by local leaders known as pirs. There is little tension in Afghanistan between Sufi orders and the ulama, which is unusual among Islamic countries. Afghans in general respect Sufi leaders for their learning, their special powers to bestow blessings, and their ability to serve as objective mediators in tribal disputes.

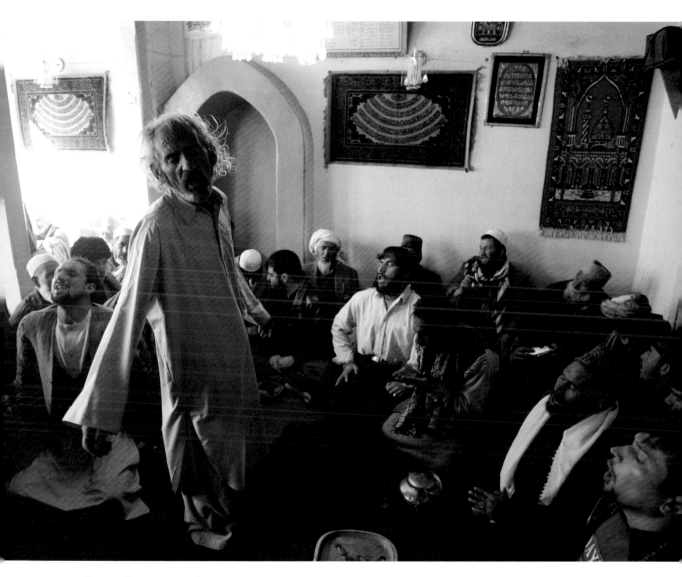

Sufi Muslims worship at a mosque in Kabul. Sufism is a mystical philosophy within Islam in which devout believers attempt to draw closer to God through music, chanting, and dancing.

Many Sufis describe their mystical experiences through poetry. The most famous Afghan Sufi poet is Jalal al-Din Muhammad Rumi (1207–1273), who founded the Sufi order of whirling dervishes, whose spinning dance was meant to simulate the universe.

Islam in Daily Life

The mosque has historically been the center of village and neighborhood life in Afghanistan. It is the site of the most basic holy day in Islam, which occurs every Friday, when Muslims gather at the mosque for the daily noon prayer. The mosque also is the center for religious celebrations and community meetings and provides shelter for travelers.

The most important Islamic leader in daily life is the mullah. Any man who can recite the Qur'an in Arabic can be a mullah. The mullah offers the sermon and prayers at Friday worship, marriages, and funerals. He also teaches Islamic law to the local population and uses Islamic law to mediate in local disputes. In addition, a mullah may be asked to provide help in many other types of community matters, such as water disputes or family disagreements.

Only men are required to attend the communal noon prayer on Friday; if women attend, they are usually separated from the men behind a curtain or in a side room. The mosque leader directs the believers in prayer as they face a niche pointing in the direction of Mecca, Islam's holiest city. After praying, believers listen as the mosque leader preaches a short message based on a verse from the Qur'an. Afterward, people visit with one another at the mosque.

Like Muslims around the world, Afghan Muslims make the five pillars of Islam an integral part of their life. These include the Islamic profession of faith ("There is no god but Allah and Muhammad is the messenger of Allah"); prayer, to be offered five times each day; almsgiving, which obligates Muslims to give charity to the poor; daily fasting during the holy month of Ramadan; and pilgrimage to Mecca in Saudi Arabia at least once in a lifetime (for all Muslims who are physically and financially able).

Aside from fasting during Ramadan, the daily prayers are the most visible sign of Muslim faith throughout Afghanistan. The prayers occur at dawn, noon or early afternoon, mid-afternoon, dusk, and early evening. Muslims must perform a ritual cleansing of different parts of the body before praying. The call to prayer is issued by the mosque **muezzin**, though it may be recorded and issued over loudspeakers in larger Afghan cities.

Many Afghan customs actually date back to the pre-Islamic era. The Pashtun code of honor, for example, commands avenging murder, even against other Muslims, which contradicts the Qur'an. Muslims throughout Afghanistan also revere "saints" of the faith, a practice forbidden in Islam. They make pilgrimages to shrines of beloved Islamic leaders and ask the deceased to intercede with God in cases of health or personal problems. It is also a common practice for Afghans to seek protection from evil by carrying amulets containing quotations from the Qur'an.

Afghan workers use buckets of mud to restore the tomb of Timur Shah, Afghanistan's second king, which was built in 1817. Today, Afghanistan is rebuilding from decades of war, thanks to financial help from dozens of countries, the United Nations, and hundreds of non-governmental organizations.

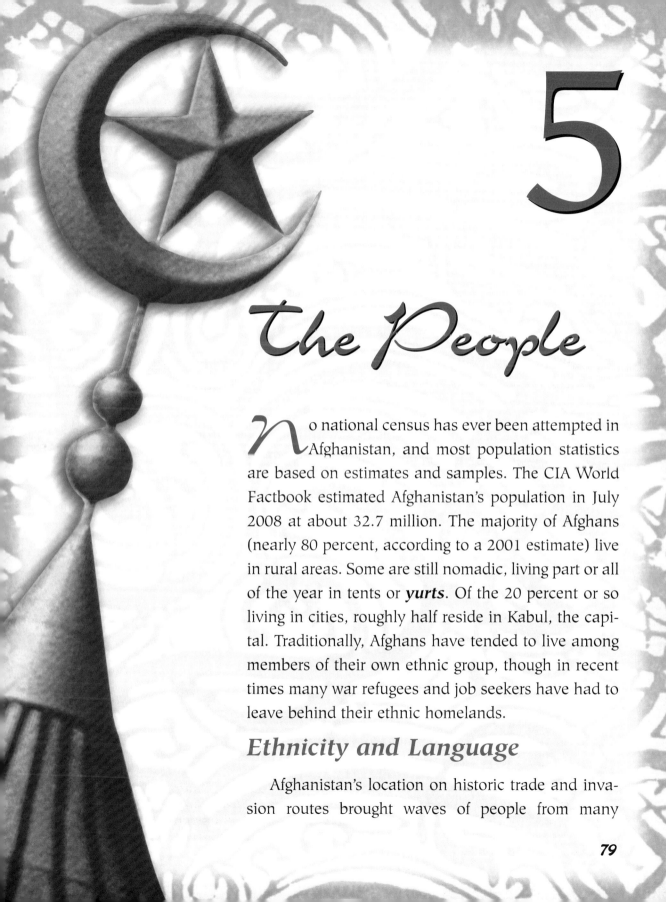

5

The People

No national census has ever been attempted in Afghanistan, and most population statistics are based on estimates and samples. The CIA World Factbook estimated Afghanistan's population in July 2008 at about 32.7 million. The majority of Afghans (nearly 80 percent, according to a 2001 estimate) live in rural areas. Some are still nomadic, living part or all of the year in tents or **yurts**. Of the 20 percent or so living in cities, roughly half reside in Kabul, the capital. Traditionally, Afghans have tended to live among members of their own ethnic group, though in recent times many war refugees and job seekers have had to leave behind their ethnic homelands.

Ethnicity and Language

Afghanistan's location on historic trade and invasion routes brought waves of people from many different regions through the country and led to its current patchwork of ethnic and linguistic groups. Today Afghanistan is home to approximately 20 main ethnic groups and more than 30 languages.

Although Afghanistan means "land of the Afghans," and although the Pashtuns sometimes refer to themselves as "Afghans," the British bestowed the country's name without reference to any particular ethnic identity. Indeed, Afghans identify primarily by their ethnicity rather than their nationality, though their common devotion to Islam and their dislike of foreign invaders have fueled a sense of national unity.

Pashtuns are the largest of the main ethnic groups, accounting for some 42 percent of the population. They live primarily in southern and eastern Afghanistan, though Pashtun groups are found throughout the country. Many Pashtuns also live in northwestern Pakistan, and Pastuns refer to their collective lands as Pashtunistan. Pashtuns speak Pashtu, an Indo-European language that is distantly related to English. Usually farmers or nomads, Pashtuns have traditionally been the most powerful ethnic group in the country. Pashtun legend has it that all Pashtuns are descendants of Qais, one of the prophet Muhammad's companions. The two

Pashtunwali, the traditional code of the Pashtun for 1,000 years or more, focuses on honor. It is encouraged and enforced by tribal elders and passed from one generation to the next. Central to the code are three principles: showing hospitality (*melmastia*) to all visitors, regardless of who they are and without any hope of reward; seeking justice, including through blood feud (*badal*) to avenge a wrong, regardless of the passage of time; and resuming peaceful relations between feuding parties (*nanawatey*), which also involves granting refuge to any who seek it.

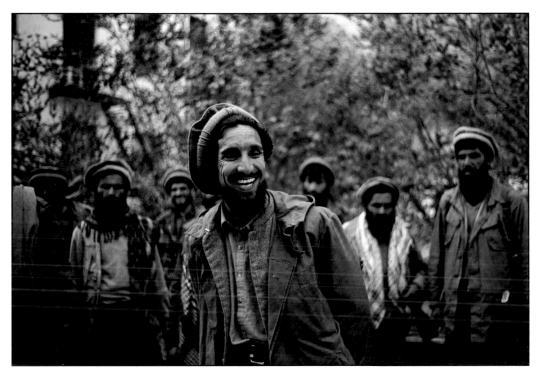

Ahmed Shah Masood, commander of the Northern Alliance militia, is pictured laughing with some of his men. Masood, an ethnic Tajik, was assassinated by the Taliban in September 2001.

most prominent Pashtun tribes are the Ghilzais and the Durranis (known before 1747 as the Abdalis), from which came the royal line of Afghanistan's monarchs. The Pashtuns are a proud people who still live by a code of conduct that emphasizes honor.

Tajiks, who make up Afghanistan's second-largest ethnic group, are closely related to the majority population in neighboring Tajikistan. They are concentrated in and around Herat, a provincial capital in the west, and in northeastern Afghanistan. Tajiks speak Dari (Afghan Persian), also an Indo-European language, which is the most widely spoken language in the country. It is the language of Afghan literature, is commonly used in business and higher education, and dominates in Afghan cities. Tajiks are sometimes farmers, though many are urban-dwelling craftspeople or merchants.

The People of Afghanistan

Population: 32,738,376
Ethnic groups: Pashtun, 42%; Tajik, 27%; Hazara, 9%; Uzbek, 9%; Aimak, 4%; Turkmen, 3%; Baloch, 2%; other, 4%
Religions: Sunni Muslim, 80%; Shia Muslim, 19%; other, 1%
Languages: Pashtu (official), 35%; Afghan Persian (Dari), 50%; Turkic languages (primarily Uzbek and Turkmen), 11%; 30 minor languages (primarily Balochi and Pashai), 4%. There is much bilingualism.
Age structure:
   0–14 years: 44.6%
   15–64 years: 53%
   65 years and over: 2.4%
Population growth rate: 2.626% (does not account for the impact of recent warfare)
Birth rate: 45.82 births/1,000 population
Death rate: 19.56 deaths/1,000 population
Infant mortality rate: 154.67 deaths/1,000 live births
Life expectancy at birth:
   total population: 44.21 years
   male: 44.04 years
   female: 44.39 years
Total fertility rate: 6.58 children born/woman
Literacy: 28.1% (2000 est.)

All figures are 2008 estimates unless otherwise indicated.
Source: Adapted from CIA World Factbook, 2008.

Uzbeks in Afghanistan are concentrated in the north. While an ethnic Uzbek population has existed within the borders of present-day Afghanistan for centuries, many Uzbeks emigrated from Central Asia in the 1920s and 1930s, as the Soviet Union consolidated its hold on the region. Afghanistan's Uzbeks are primarily farmers, though many also raise horses or Karakul sheep.

The Turkmen, another group with ties to Central Asia, are noted sheep breeders and carpet weavers. As with the Uzbeks, many Turkmen moved south into Afghanistan from neighboring Turkmenistan to escape Soviet-era repression.

The Hazaras live primarily in Afghanistan's central mountain ranges. Most are Imami Shiites, which has caused tension with other Afghans, especially the Pashtuns. The Hazaras were severely persecuted by the Taliban. Many Hazaras farm or raise sheep; others have migrated to the cities to take service jobs. The Hazaras speak an archaic form of Persian.

The Nuristanis live in an isolated mountainous region in northeastern Afghanistan. They converted to Islam only in the late 1800s; before then, they practiced a form of polytheism that involved ancestor worship. The Nuristanis speak several Indo-European dialects, and many have light skin and blond or red hair—leading to speculation that their ancestors came from Europe. Nuristani tradition holds that they are descendants of Alexander the Great and his army, which conquered the region in the fourth century B.C.E.

In the face of Afghanistan's ethnic diversity, forging unity and a national identity has remained a challenge since the country came into being in the mid-1700s. Afghans have managed to put aside their ethnic differences to confront an outside threat—as with the Soviet occupation, for example—but this unity has not lasted after the threat is removed. When the Soviets departed, for instance, divisions quickly reappeared. Most of the Taliban were Pashtuns, while the Northern Alliance was dominated by Tajiks, Uzbeks, and Hazaras. A central task for the new Afghan government is to build support among all ethnic groups for a united Afghanistan.

Islam continues to be an important factor in this appeal to unity, though tensions between the Sunni majority and the Shia minority remain.

Village, Town, and City Life

Smaller villages in Afghanistan usually do not have schools, stores, or government offices, and villagers must travel to town **bazaars** for supplies or buy them from peddlers or nomads. The village mosque serves as the community center.

Village men typically work in the fields, joined by the women during the harvest. Some village men also perform part-time jobs—doing construction or repairing shoes, for example—between harvest and planting time. Nomads often serve as an important link to the outside world, bringing

An Afghan woman's fiancé and grandmother place rings on her fingers during an engagement ceremony.

news as they pass through villages on their way from highland grazing grounds to their winter camps in the lowlands. The nomads buy supplies like grains and nuts from the villagers, while the villagers buy goods like carpets, cloth, sugar, spices, and tea from the nomads.

In Afghanistan, as in other countries, cities are centers of commerce as well as magnets for people seeking economic opportunities. A handful of larger Afghan cities have modern sectors for manufacturing and business, but elsewhere the bazaar remains the center of economic life in cities and towns. The bazaar is divided into streets for different craftspeople (coppersmiths, leather workers, and shoemakers, for example) and food vendors (such as bakers, butchers, and fishmongers).

Marriage

Following long-held custom, Afghans are expected to marry within their own ethnic group. However, this practice has changed somewhat in recent times, as Afghans have increasingly moved outside their ethnic territories and forged relationships with other ethnic groups. Marriages between first and second cousins are still highly sought after, and the competition between male cousins for brides remains the theme of many songs and folktales.

Each marriage is arranged publicly between two families and has traditionally involved a marriage contract that specifies the transfer of money or property from the groom's family to the bride's family, known as a bride-price. This does not follow Islamic law, which requires a payment of money or property directly to the bride to ensure her financial stability in the event of divorce. The need for a large transfer of property at marriage also means that young girls are sometimes married to older men, who have had time to accumulate more goods. Most Afghans, however, marry in their late teens or twenties.

The marriage contract also outlines the dowry the bride will bring to the marriage, consisting of clothing, linens, and household items. In urban settings, the dowry may also include kitchen appliances such as stoves and refrigerators.

Polygyny is permitted, but its practice has declined significantly in recent decades as poverty has increased. Divorce is still very uncommon, and in the case of infertility, the family considers it far more acceptable for a man to marry a second wife than to divorce the first. The ancient custom known as the levirate, in which a widow is married to a member of her deceased husband's family, is explicitly forbidden in the Qur'an, and by the 1960s it was rare in Afghanistan. However, after the Soviet invasion, the practice was taken up again to provide security for the high number of war widows.

The traditional wedding celebration lasts three days. On the first day, the two families gather and socialize. On the second day, the groom leads a procession of his male relatives, accompanied by musicians and dancers, while the women prepare the bride's hair and clothing. On the third day, the bride and groom wear traditional dress for a feast, followed by the signing of the marriage contract and the actual marriage ceremony, officiated by the local mullah. During the ceremony, the bride and groom read a special wedding recitation together and decorate each other's little fingers with henna and a piece of embroidered cloth. Wedding guests then shower sugared almonds on the newlyweds. In urban settings, the three-day celebration is now often condensed into one day, and the couple often wears Western rather than traditional dress.

The Communist leaders of the 1970s and 1980s prohibited high bride-prices, child and forced marriages, and the levirate. The Taliban overturned these laws, however, and it is unclear how these practices will be regulated under the country's new government.

Family Life

The extended family has historically been the major economic and social unit in Afghan society. Families pay great respect to the elders within their intergenerational families. The oldest male has authority, followed by the other males in the family. On most domestic matters, however, older women have authority; the daughters-in-law and unmarried daughters are under the control of the mother.

Gender roles have traditionally been very rigid in Afghanistan, though they differ in rural and urban settings. In rural areas, women often perform key roles in providing for the family (weaving carpets or assisting in the harvest, for example). In urban areas, women have traditionally been more confined to their homes, taking care of domestic matters. Women in

With the end of Taliban rule in 2002 and passage of the constitution in 2004, women in Afghanistan received greater freedom. However, both Afghan tradition and Islam as practiced in Afghanistan lead to the continued subordination of women.

urban areas began to go outside the home and work in the 1950s, but the Taliban forbade women to attend school, hold a job, or even leave their homes without a male relative. Since the overthrow of the Taliban, some urban women are once again attending school and pursuing careers, and the country's new constitution guarantees equal rights for men and women. In most cases, however, men still hold the traditional role of making crucial decisions about education, careers, and marriage for the women in their families.

Afghans traditionally mark the birth of a child with a celebration involving gifts, music, and a naming ceremony. Sons are highly prized, and birth ceremonies have historically been more elaborate for boys than for girls. From around the age of four, boys begin to work in the fields and look after livestock, while girls look after younger children and help with cleaning and cooking. Afghan boys are considered adults by the age of 12, and most girls are expected to fully participate in domestic work by the age of 9 or 10.

Inheritance is **patrilineal**, following the Qur'an, and the ratio of inheritance is two to one in favor of males. A widow therefore receives one-third of her sons' shares. In practice, women are often denied their part of the inheritance, which causes conflict within families.

Village Afghans typically live in a mud-brick house or a walled compound made up of several houses. In most houses, the rooms surround a rectangular courtyard used for cooking and socializing. Married sons usually live in the family compound with their parents, while daughters go to live with their husband's families. Nomadic Afghans live in tents arranged like family compounds, while urban Afghans live in houses or apartment buildings.

Afghans have a long tradition of being extremely generous to guests. Hospitality is so highly valued, in fact, that any lack of social etiquette on the part of a family member threatens the honor and reputation of the entire family.

Dress

Though Western apparel is appearing in Kabul again after the fall of the Taliban, both men and women have traditionally dressed modestly in Afghanistan, which means covering the entire body from neck to foot. The typical clothing is loose and comfortable. Most men wear a long cotton tunic over baggy pants (an outfit called a *sharwar kami*), with a wide sash tied around the waist. Many also wear a turban, often indicating their tribal identity by tying their turban in a certain way. Women also wear a *sharwar kami* or long dress over trousers. Even after the Taliban's ouster, many women have continued to wear the burqa by choice, but many rural women and more educated urban women wear no veil at all or opt for the chador, a large piece of material that covers the head and chest and falls below the knees.

Health Care

In various measures of health and human welfare, Afghanistan ranks near the very bottom of the world's nations. For example, Afghans' life expectancy at birth was estimated at 44.21 years in 2008; that is more than 20 years below the world average (67.2 years). For every 1,000 Afghan babies born, about 155 infants die before their first birthday—a staggering infant mortality rate that is almost four times the world average (42.64). A number of factors contribute to these grim statistics: shortages of medical facilities and doctors; poor sanitation; severe malnutrition; lack of immunization; the prevalence of diseases such as measles, cholera, and tuberculosis; and even land mines left over from the country's past conflicts. Overall, the nation's health problems are more severe in rural areas, where the patient-to-doctor ratio is very high. As bad as current conditions are, in many respects the situation was even worse—especially for women—under the Taliban. Because of their extreme beliefs about gender

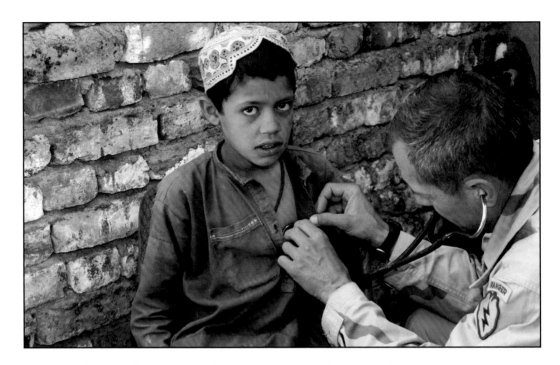

A U.S. military doctor examines a young Afghan boy. Since 2001 the United States and other countries have worked to improve medical facilities and access to health care in Afghanistan.

roles and segregation of the sexes, the Taliban prohibited female doctors from practicing and male doctors from examining female patients, which left most women without any medical care whatsoever.

In conjunction with international aid organizations, however, Afghanistan's government is now working hard to provide medical personnel and basic health services for all Afghans, especially in rural areas. Vaccinations have risen dramatically, slowing the spread of diseases; clinics and trained midwives are increasingly available for mothers-to-be; and victims of land mines are receiving artificial limbs.

Education System and Literacy

By the late 1800s, the Afghan government sought to extend secular education to rural areas as a way to demonstrate the compatibility of

Islam and modernization. But the only education available for most rural Afghans was in madrassas, which were run by local mosques and open only to boys. The madrassas taught Islamic values through study of the Qur'an and **Hadith**.

Public education was established for boys in 1903 and girls in 1924. In 1935 it was declared universal, mandatory, and free. Kabul University was founded in 1932; nine other colleges opened by 1967. Despite these measures, however, most Afghan children did not receive an education. Reasons included a lack of adequate facilities in rural areas; the widespread belief, particularly among rural populations, that education was unnecessary; the need for poor children to be kept at home to work; and the opposition of some Islamic leaders to education for girls. In practice, education remained primarily for upper-class urban children.

In the 1980s Soviet forces obliterated many Afghan villages, which not only destroyed schools but also produced a stream of refugees, including teachers and students. On the other hand, thousands of Afghan teenagers received a Soviet-style education in Soviet institutions during this period. By late 1981, only two years into the Soviet occupation, Afghans already represented the largest student contingent from any developing country in the U.S.S.R. (8,700 of a total of about 72,000). By the end of 1983 an estimated 20,000 young Afghan men and women had gone to the Soviet Union for civilian and military training and further education. That legacy is still felt today, as a large portion of the pool of available secular teachers are Afghan men and women trained in the U.S.S.R.

The rule of the Taliban helps explain why that remains the case more than a decade and a half since the Soviets withdrew from Afghanistan. With their Islamic fundamentalist worldview, the Taliban emphasized religious rather than secular education. They also prohibited all education for girls over age 12 and forbade women to teach. By 1996 Afghanistan had a higher illiteracy rate—for both men and women—than any country in

Students participate in a class discussion at the Tajwarsultana School for Girls in Kabul. The school, destroyed during the Taliban era, was rebuilt in 2002. Today, more than 4,300 young women attend the school in three shifts.

Asia. By 2000 the country's literacy rate was one of the lowest in the world—an estimated 28 percent overall. Perhaps not surprisingly, the literacy rate varied dramatically by gender: while an estimated 43 percent of males age 15 and older could read and write, the figure for females stood at only 13 percent.

As Afghanistan's political and social situation becomes more stable following the establishment of a post-Taliban government, children throughout the country are slowly returning to primary school (as of 2004, only grades one to six were compulsory). Many obstacles to school attendance persist, however. Some girls are still prevented by their families from attending school. In addition, inadequate facilities and insufficient funds to pay teachers remain problems, especially in rural areas.

Arts and Culture

The arts and culture of Afghanistan reflect complex encounters between diverse cultures, religions, and ethnic groups. Through the centuries, Afghans have especially loved poetry and folktales, and these remain vital in a society with few televisions or radios. Many Afghans read poetry regularly and can recite or write a verse to commemorate any occasion. Poems often honor heroic virtues, religious piety, or romantic love. Among the most famous Afghan poets are the 13th-century Sufi poet Jalal al-Din Muhammad Rumi, whose central work is the six-volume *Masnavi-ye Manavi* (Spiritual Couplets), and Kaushal Khan Khattak, the 17th-century Pashtun "warrior-poet" who encouraged Afghans to unite against the Mughals.

Educated adults read and recite Persian literature. The 10th-century *Shahnama* (Book of Kings), the national epic of Iran composed by the poet Ferdowsi, is especially important to Dari-speaking Afghans. Children are often told animal fables from *Kalilah and Dimnah,* written in India more than 2,500 years ago and probably the basis for *Aesop's Fables.*

Though they were banned by the Taliban, music and dance are also very important to Afghan culture. Among the more popular instruments are a plucked mouth harp known as the *chang,* a variety of drums, and the six-stringed *rohab,* considered the predecessor of the Western violin and cello. The oldest musical traditions, found in the north and west, have ties to Iran and Central Asia, while in southern and eastern Afghanistan musical styles are inspired by Indian music. Several forms of folk music are used as accompaniments to poems.

Public dancing is a common feature of all Afghan celebrations. At most such events, Afghans perform the national dance, called the *atan,* in which dancers gather in a large circle, clap their hands, and move their feet quickly to the rhythm of the music.

Afghanistan is home to plentiful architectural remnants of earlier civilizations, including Greek and Buddhist shrines as well as monasteries, arches, temples, and forts. Many mosques are noted for their domes and minarets. The 15th-century Musalla minarets in Herat are the country's most famous.

Many mosques and Islamic shrines are covered with tile work, an ancient art form developed in the Middle East. The 15th-century Shrine of Hazrat Ali in Mazar-e-Sharif, for example, is covered with intricate blue tile mosaics fashioned to form pictures of flowers. In addition to tile work, Afghan artisans are also known for their calligraphy, Persian-style woven carpets, and elaborate hand embroidery.

It is estimated that approximately 80 percent of Afghanistan's art works were lost, stolen, destroyed, or damaged during the recent decades of warfare. After prohibiting all statues of non-Islamic gods and all depictions of humans and animals in art, the Taliban dynamited the great ancient Buddhas carved into a rock face in the Bamiyan Valley (the largest representations of Buddha in the world) and destroyed most of the statues in the National Museum in Kabul. The museum was also repeatedly hit by rockets during fighting in the 1990s, and an estimated two-thirds of its collection was looted.

Reports indicate that artifacts from the country's vulnerable archaeological and cultural heritage sites continue to be removed and sold illegally, despite the efforts of government officials and international organizations to stop this activity. Efforts are also under way to reconstruct damaged artifacts like the Bamiyan Buddhas and to secure the return of the country's looted treasures.

Sports

A favorite sport in northern Afghanistan is *buzkashi* ("grab the goat"), an ancient game widely believed to have developed in Central Asia. It is most commonly played on the newly harvested wheat and barley fields in late summer or early fall and again in spring around the time of the New Year's celebration (Nawruz). While Tajiks and Turkmen also play buzkashi, the Uzbeks have long been the champions of the game. Teams of 10 men on horseback gather in a circle for the game, in which the headless carcass of a goat or calf is thrown to the ground in the center. The riders then rush in, each trying to lift the carcass onto his horse. To score a goal, the rider with the carcass then must gallop through the other riders—all equipped with whips— to a goal point, usually about a mile away, and back to the starting point. Both horses and buzkashi masters are highly trained.

A type of wrestling known as *pahlwani* is also very popular and often occurs alongside buzkashi matches. The goal of pahlwani is simple: a

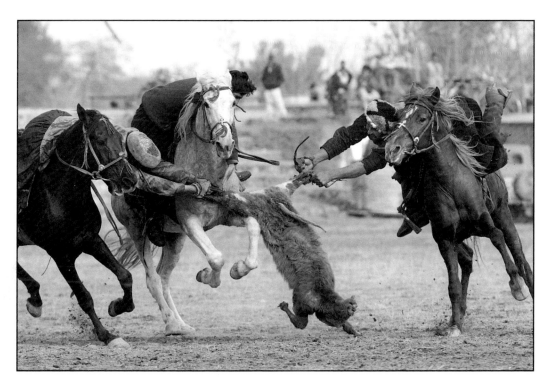

Afghan horsemen fight over the carcass of a headless calf during a spirited game of *buzkashi*.

wrestler tries to pin his opponent's shoulders to the ground without touching his legs. Competition between village teams is common.

Western sports like soccer and field hockey are also played, and children enjoy flying kites as well as a game called *buzul-bazi*, which is similar to marbles. Children and adults play card games and chess.

Cuisine

Afghanistan's culinary tradition is as rich as its history. Ingredients from different cultures include spices from India; mint and yogurt from Persia; and pasta from China and Mongolia.

Afghans rely on grains as the staple of their diet, using up to 20 varieties of rice. Other food basics include bread, cheese, eggs, *maast* (a tart yogurt), nuts such as pistachios and almonds, numerous fruits and vegetables, and tea. Afghans also use local meats, slaughtering livestock according to Islamic dietary law *(halal)*.

The vegetables used most commonly in various combinations include carrots, raisins, spinach, squash, eggplant, potatoes, and tomatoes. These are combined with lamb, chicken, and beef when meat is used. Afghans use fresh herbs, especially mint, to season their dishes, as well as spices like garam masala, saffron, cinnamon, cardamom, coriander, and ginger. Poppy seeds, sesame seeds, and green and red chilies are also used as seasoning.

Pilau, rice served with meat and vegetables, is common throughout the country. An important traditional dish is *kabuli pilau*, which includes chunks of lamb beneath brown rice topped with carrot strips, raisins, almonds, and pistachios. Pilau and other meals are usually accompanied by maast, a mixture of pickled vegetables (*torshi*), and hot chili sauce.

Another common Afghan dish is *kabab*, small cubes of meat skewered with vegetables like onions and tomatoes and grilled. *Kofta kabab* includes minced meat ground with onions, while *shami kabab* is made of minced meat mixed with mashed potatoes and raw eggs.

Another popular dish, which looks somewhat like Italian ravioli, is *aushak*, scallion-filled dumplings topped with yogurt, meat sauce, and mint. A similar pastry dish is *mantu*, a dumpling filled with meat and onion.

Most meals are accompanied by bread and rice. Rice is usually served plain, though for more formal meals, it is cooked into a pilau. The most common bread is *naan*, a flat, oblong bread made from whatever grain is available. Bread is traditionally baked daily in a clay pot buried in the ground over coals (a *tandur*) or on a heated stone.

Dessert often includes local fruits such as melons, apples, and apricots. A popular cooked dessert is *firni*, a milk pudding topped with pistachios.

When Afghans gather for meals, they wash their hands together and then sit on large cushions, share food from large ceramic platters placed on a cloth spread over a carpet, and eat with the fingers of their right hands. Food is integral to the hospitality shown throughout Afghanistan. Guests are routinely offered tea and are given the best food when a meal is served, even if this means family members must go without.

Holidays and Festivals

Afghans join Muslims around the world in celebrating their annual religious holidays. These holidays are based on the Islamic lunar calendar, which means that the dates on the Western calendar vary from year to year.

The ninth month of the Islamic calendar is Ramadan, the month of fasting (*ruzah* in Afghanistan). Each day during Ramadan, Afghan Muslims rise to eat a predawn meal and then fast until after sunset, when they eat dates or raisins to break their fast, followed by pilau and tea. The times for beginning and ending the daily fast are announced from mosques, though in Kabul, a cannon is fired to mark these times. The daily fast is a time for prayer, and the evening is a time for special events such as nightly Ramadan prayers and Qur'an recitations. Toward the end of Ramadan, Afghans who are financially able follow the Muslim principle of voluntary charity (*sadaqah*) and give money, gifts, and food to those in need.

The end of Ramadan is celebrated with the fast-breaking festival known as Eid al-Fitr, when Afghans joyously celebrate the spiritual enlightenment gained during Ramadan. This is a time for saying prayers, wearing new clothes, and feasting with family and friends.

Muslim men raise a *jonda* pole outside the Karti Sakhi Shrine in Kabul. The *jonda* pole is erected each year for the Nawruz celebration in Afghanistan; it remains up for 40 days as a symbol of the renewal of life that occurs in the spring.

Another important Muslim festival is Eid al-Adha, the Feast of Sacrifice, which occurs during the annual hajj, when Muslim pilgrims travel to Islam's holiest city, Mecca, in Saudi Arabia. The hajj occurs during the 12th month of the Islamic year and is marked by a series of rituals performed in Mecca and surrounding areas. Afghan families who can afford it slaughter a sheep for Eid al-Adha, with one-third going to the family, one-third to relatives, and the remaining third to the poor. The festival usually lasts four days and includes a gift exchange among family and friends.

Other Muslim occasions marked in Afghanistan include Mawlid-an-Nabi, the prophet Muhammad's birthday; and the 10 days of mourning called Muharram, observed by Shiites to mark the death of their martyr Hussein, Ali's son and the prophet Muhammad's grandson. Shiites also celebrate dates associated with their Imams.

The most important non-Muslim holiday is New Year's Day, known as Nawruz ("new day"), which is celebrated on the spring equinox. A modern version of ancient Zoroastrian renewal festivals, it is also widely celebrated in neighboring Central Asian countries. It usually lasts two days and involves traditional games, music, drama, and food. Parents often give gifts to their children at Nawruz, and it is also a time for visiting the graves of ancestors and giving charity.

The most prominent national holidays in Afghanistan include Independence Day (August 18), which marks Afghanistan's independence from the British after the end of the Third Anglo-Afghan War in 1919. Other national holidays include Revolution Day on April 27 and Labor Day on May 1.

The Shrine of Hazrat Ali in Mazar-e-Sharif, known for its ornate tile work, was commissioned in 1481. An earlier shrine, built in 1136, was destroyed when Genghis Khan and the Mongols sacked Mazar-e-Sharif in 1220.

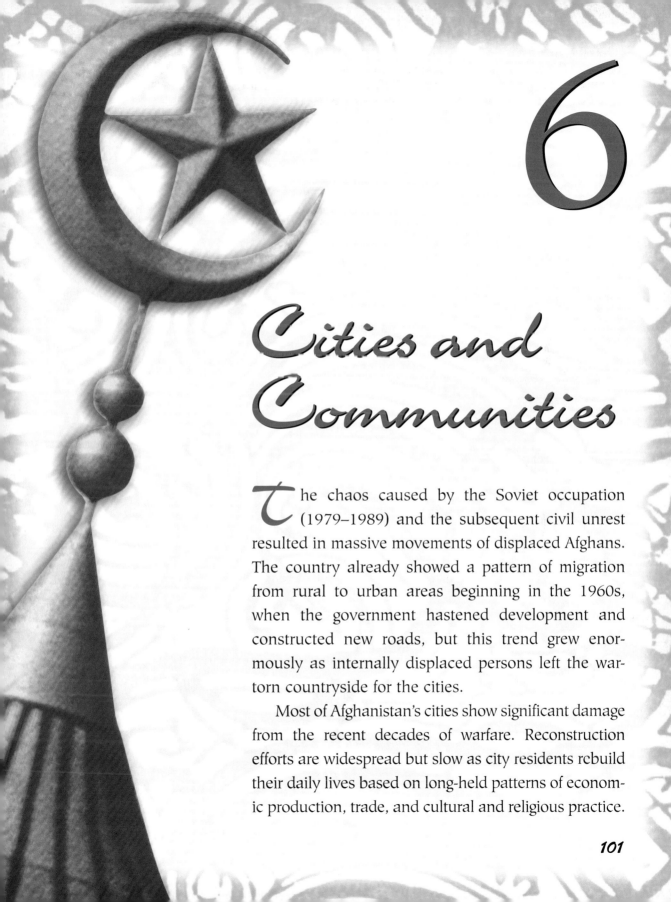

6

Cities and Communities

The chaos caused by the Soviet occupation (1979–1989) and the subsequent civil unrest resulted in massive movements of displaced Afghans. The country already showed a pattern of migration from rural to urban areas beginning in the 1960s, when the government hastened development and constructed new roads, but this trend grew enormously as internally displaced persons left the war-torn countryside for the cities.

Most of Afghanistan's cities show significant damage from the recent decades of warfare. Reconstruction efforts are widespread but slow as city residents rebuild their daily lives based on long-held patterns of economic production, trade, and cultural and religious practice.

Kabul

Located at the crossroads of major trade routes in east-central Afghanistan, Kabul is Afghanistan's largest city, capital, and economic and cultural center. It sits on both sides of the Kabul River high in a mountain valley near the strategic Khyber Pass. At an elevation of 5,876 feet (1,791 meters), it is one of the highest capital cities in the world.

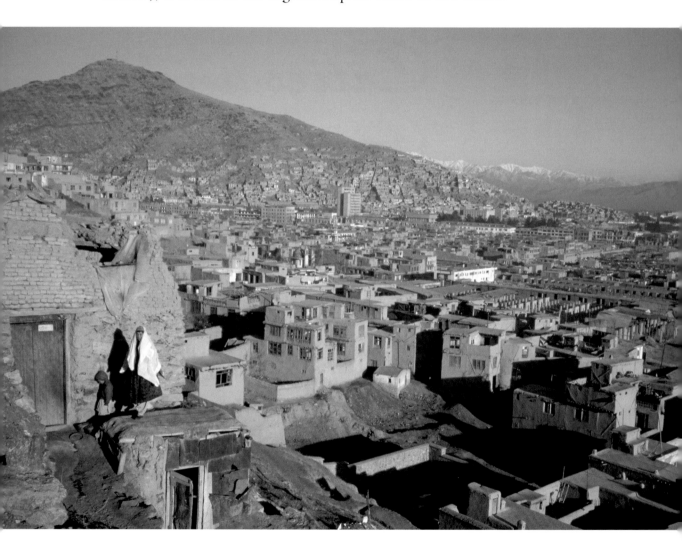

A view of Kabul, Afghanistan's capital and largest city.

Though it has been destroyed and rebuilt several times, Kabul is one of the world's most ancient cities, founded more than 3,000 years ago. The Rig-Veda (Indian scriptures dating to approximately 1500 B.C.E.) mentions Kabul, and the city was known by ancient geographers and mathematicians. The Afghan cities Ghazni and Herat achieved prominence first, but then Babur made Kabul the capital of the Mughal Empire in 1504, and it remained an important Mughal city until its capture by Nadir Shah of Iran in 1738. Kabul was included when Afghanistan became an independent state in 1747, and in 1776 the capital was shifted from Kandahar to Kabul. The city then became central to the British, Persian, and Russian struggle for control of the Khyber Pass, and British troops occupied it twice (1839–1842 and 1879–1880).

Long a center of trade, Kabul expanded into an industrial center beginning in the 1940s. In the 1970s Kabul University established partnerships with academic institutions from around the world to increase its programs and faculty.

Kabul's fortunes took a different turn in 1979, however, when it became the center of the Soviet occupation. Though the city went largely unscathed by fighting during the decade of Soviet control, it became the site of extreme conflict between rival mujahedin factions after the Soviets withdrew. Many sections of Kabul, especially in its western and southern parts, were damaged or destroyed.

While many residents fled the fighting in Kabul, others flooded into the city to escape fighting in the countryside or were later forced by the Taliban to move into Kabul, where they put a severe strain on the city's resources. The population of Kabul stood at roughly 1.4 million in 1989, but by 2006 it was estimated to have reached 2.5 million. Since the establishment of the transitional government in 2002, the city has been teeming with returning Afghan refugees and large groups of international aid workers. It has also been bustling with renewed economic activity and

> Among Kabul's most interesting cultural attractions is Babur's Gardens, which were laid out by Babur himself on hillside terraces. The gardens include Babur's grave and a white mosque designed by the architect of the Taj Mahal in India. Long a favorite picnicking spot for Kabul residents, the gardens were badly damaged by fighting in the 1990s. They are now being restored.

reconstruction projects. Tajiks are the majority in Kabul, though Pashtuns make up a sizeable minority.

Kabul's industry was severely hampered and its infrastructure badly damaged in the fighting of the 1990s. It was the center of the Afghan carpet trade until the mujahedin capture of the city in 1992 led to a mass exodus of Afghan weavers into Pakistan. The weavers have been returning to Afghanistan in large numbers since 2002, however, and the Kabul carpet trade is recovering. Other industries include rayon and wool mills, food-processing plants, furniture factories, and marble and lapis lazuli works. Efforts are planned or under way to reconstruct the roads that connect Kabul to the other Afghan provinces, Pakistan, and Central Asia. Kabul International Airport, riddled with land mines, has also been slated by international donors for reconstruction.

Kabul University closed because of warfare in 1992; heavy fighting among mujahedin factions further damaged or destroyed most of its buildings. After the fall of the Taliban, however, the university partially reopened, and plans are under way for reconstruction.

The more modern areas of Kabul contain government and commercial buildings and streets congested with trucks, cars, buses, horse carts, camels, and donkeys. In contrast, the narrow, crooked streets of the old city on the south bank of the Kabul River lead to flat-roofed houses and the city's many colorful bazaars.

Chief historical attractions in Kabul include Babur's Gardens, the city's old walls, and Bala Hissar, a fortress dating back to the Ephthalites in the fifth century. Many cultural points of interest in the city are in disrepair and awaiting reconstruction. Among the most important of these are the octagonal tomb of King Timur Shah and the Id Gah Mosque, the focus of national and religious celebrations. The National Museum in Kabul was largely destroyed by civil conflict and the Taliban, but it is currently being restored.

Kandahar

With an estimated 2006 population of nearly 325,000 Kandahar is Afghanistan's third-largest city. Located in the southern part of the country about the same distance from Kabul and Herat, it sits on a plain along the Tarnak River. Kandahar was the first capital of modern Afghanistan, and it ranks with Peshawar, Pakistan, as the most important cities of the Pashtun people.

Kandahar was founded under the rule of the Macedonian conqueror Alexander the Great, but it later fell to the Buddhist Mauryan Empire and then to the Muslim Arabs. Babur took control of Kandahar in the 1500s, and the Mughals and the Persian Safavids fought over Kandahar into the 1600s because of its location on trade routes to Kabul, Herat, and India. When Ahmad Shah Durrani created a newly independent Afghanistan in 1747, he named Kandahar the capital, and in 1761 he designed the plans for modern Kandahar. During the two Anglo-Afghan wars of the 1800s, the British army occupied the city, and the Soviets used its airport as a military base during their occupation. The Soviets bombed southern sections of Kandahar extensively, and it remains ridden with land mines.

After the Soviet occupation ended, rival mujahedin factions fought for control of Kandahar. Finally, in 1994, it became the first city captured by Taliban forces. The Pashtun citizens of Kandahar generally welcomed the

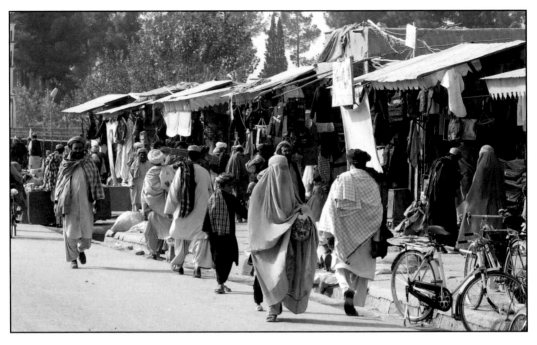

A street scene in Kandahar. Afghanistan's second-largest city is also a major center for trade.

Taliban, who brought some stability after long years of chaos, and the Taliban treated Kandahar as their capital even after they captured Kabul. Kandahar was the last major city to fall to the American-led military coalition in 2001, and tension with Western military forces and the national government still runs high in the city. An assassination attempt was made against President Karzai in Kandahar in 2002, and resistance fighters continue to stage attacks on foreign and Afghan aid workers there.

Even though Kandahar was a center of Taliban support, business in the city has improved since the Taliban's defeat. The city is the international aid headquarters for the region, which has brought an influx of foreigners, and the roads connecting Kandahar to Kabul, Herat, Pakistan, and Central Asia are being reconstructed. Kandahar has long been the country's central trading center, with large markets for sheep, wool, cotton, grains, fruit, and tobacco. Before the Soviet occupation, its orchards and vineyards were the most productive in Afghanistan, and the fruit was processed at plants in the city. Manufacturing in Kandahar consists largely of textiles, including wool, felt, and silk.

As in Kabul, modern Kandahar is next to the old city center, but its bazaars are roomier. The most important historical attraction in Kandahar is the tomb of Ahmad Shah Durrani, an octagonal building covered in multiple colors of tile and topped by a blue dome. Next to the tomb is the Shrine of the Cloak of the Prophet Muhammad, arguably the most important shrine in the country, which holds an important religious relic brought to Kandahar by Ahmad Shah. Also of interest is a rock engraving known as Chel Zina, which dates from the time of the Mughal Empire and lists Babur's conquests.

Mazar-e-Sharif

Mazar-e-Sharif, the capital of Balkh Province in northern Afghanistan, is located about 250 miles (400 kilometers) northwest of Kabul. With an estimated 2006 population of approximately 300,600, it is Afghanistan's fourth-largest city. Uzbeks and Tajiks dominate the population, with significant Pashtun and Hazara minorities.

Mazar rose to prominence only in the 19th century, after nearby Balkh was abandoned because of an outbreak of cholera. During the Soviet occupation, Mazar was an important base for government forces as well as various mujahedin factions. In 1992 military general Abdul Rashid Dostum rebelled against the Kabul authorities and established an independent region in north Afghanistan based in Mazar. Under Dostum's leadership, Mazar remained quiet during the fighting of the mid-1990s, but the Taliban took control briefly in 1998 and again in 1999, after which they carried out brutal reprisals against the local population. Dostum's forces joined the U.S.-supported Northern Alliance in 2001, and Mazar was the first city recaptured. Dostum then took control of the city again, but he was quickly challenged by a rival warlord, and three years later their forces continued to battle each other in the local countryside.

Mazar has long been a major trading center for Karakul wool, traditional carpets, and cotton. Farming and the raising of Karakul sheep and horses dominate the local economy, though some oil and gas exploration have occurred recently.

Mazar is home to a very important pilgrimage site for Afghan Shiites. While the larger Islamic world maintains that Ali, the cousin and son-in-law of the prophet Muhammad and the fourth Islamic caliph, is buried in Najaf, Iraq, Afghans believe he is buried in Mazar. Local legend holds that his body was excavated in a nearby village in the 12th century, but the tomb built there for Ali was destroyed by the forces of Genghis Khan. A new shrine, known as the Shrine of Hazrat Ali, was built in Mazar in the 15th century. Though little of the original decoration still exists, the shrine's blue mosaic tile and twin domes have been extensively restored. According to local tradition, the thousands of pigeons that flock in the shrine courtyard will turn white in 40 days if they remain—a sign of how holy the area is.

Charikar

Charikar, the capital of Parvan Province, lies just 30 miles (48 km) north of Kabul, and the corridor between the two cities is the most densely populated area of Afghanistan. At the time of the Soviet invasion in 1979, Charikar was a small town of about 20,000. Since the departure of the Soviets, however, the flood of displaced Afghans pouring into Kabul has overflowed into Charikar, swelling its population to more than twice that number in less than 30 years.

During the Soviet occupation, Charikar was at the center of some of the most bitter fighting. As the civil conflict of the 1990s developed, the population of Charikar rose and fell depending on the current level of security; when the Taliban captured the city in early 1996, they relocated many of its residents to Kabul to reduce pockets of resistance in the area.

Charikar sits at an altitude of about 5,300 feet (1,615 meters). The city has long been recognized for its outstanding grape vineyards. Its industries include pottery, iron, and cutlery.

Herat

The capital of Herat Province, Herat sits on the Harirud River in northwestern Afghanistan. The city is one of the largest in the country, with approximately 349,000 people by 2006 estimates; most are Tajiks.

Herat, widely considered Afghanistan's most beautiful ancient city, has a history that dates back about 2,500 years, when it was founded as the Persian town of Artacoana. Even today, unmistakable signs of the Persian culture can still be seen, though the city has felt numerous other influences as well, beginning in 330 B.C. with the conquest of the region by Alexander the Great.

Herat's strategic location on the trade route from Persia to India and the caravan route from Asia to Europe made it a coveted prize for competing empires; through the centuries it was many times conquered, destroyed, and rebuilt. The Mongols under Genghis Khan massacred

In the 15th century, Timur Lenk's son Shah Rukh made Herat the capital of the Timurid Empire and ushered in the Timurid Renaissance, a vibrant period known for its literature, music, calligraphy, miniature painting, and architecture. Shah Rukh's wife Gawhar Shad ("bright jewel") was a patron of writers, artists, and scholars and helped design the famous Musalla complex, which included minarets, a mosque, and a college.

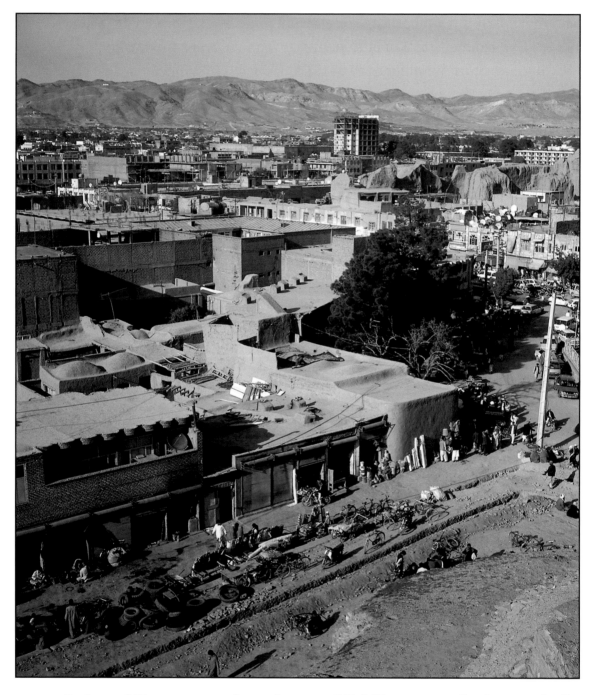

A view of Herat as seen from the top of Pai Hesar, a castle that overlooks the city. The castle was supposedly built for Alexander the Great.

almost the entire population of Herat in 1221. Timur destroyed the city in 1381; however, his son rebuilt it and made it a renowned center of culture and learning. Later, the Persians and the leaders of the newly independent Afghanistan fought over Herat, assisted by the competing imperialist powers Russia and Great Britain, until it was officially made part of Afghanistan in 1881.

Herat rebelled against the Communist government in March 1979 by massacring some 100 Soviet advisers and their dependents. The Soviets responded by bombing the city extensively in their first military action inside Afghanistan, killing several thousand civilians. After the Soviet pullout, the military commander Ismail Khan took power. In 1995 the Taliban captured Herat and took Ismail Khan prisoner, but in 2000 he managed to escape to Iran. From there he organized the recapture of Herat at the time of the U.S.-led invasion.

After that, Khan set himself up as the virtual amir of Herat. Though he managed to reestablish order and rebuild the city (largely through funding from Iran, with whose Shiite government he had developed close ties), Khan operated independently of the national government. He not only implemented strict Islamic law but also, critics charged, skimmed tax revenues for his own use. Seeking to bring regional warlords under control and reassert national authority, Hamid Karzai in September 2004 attempted to replace Khan with a governor of Herat Province, which triggered violent riots in the city of Herat. U.S. troops assisted the Afghan National Army in putting down the riots, and the new governor, Mohammed Khair Khuwa, was then successfully installed. As of 2007 Herat has been occupied by NATO peacekeeping forces that can be found in and around the city providing security.

The fertile river valley surrounding Herat is known for its orchards and vineyards, and the city is a trading center for grains, fruit, vegetables, wool, and carpets. As the largest city in western Afghanistan, Herat is the gateway for exports from Afghanistan and western Pakistan to Iran, the Middle East, and Turkmenistan. Herat's bazaars once bustled with the trade generated by passing caravans. Today, the markets offer carpets and the traditional blue glass produced by the city's glass blowers. The old city sits at the center of Herat and is home to a variety of ancient architectural styles. The newly renovated Friday Mosque, which sits at the center of the old city, has been a center of prayer and community life since the time of Zoroaster. The Pai Hesar fortress, said to date to the time of Alexander the Great, provides a vivid reminder of the city's rich history.

To the north and east of the city lie the Gazargah shrine and the remains of the Musalla minarets. The Gazargah shrine is the tomb of the famous 11th-century poet and mystic Khaja Abdullah Ansari. The Musalla minarets originally numbered 12 when they were built as part of the great Musalla complex commissioned as a center of learning and worship in the late 1400s. Historical documents point to the Musalla buildings as some of the most impressive in Asia. Earthquakes and attacks by both the British and the Russians have claimed seven of the minarets, but the remaining five are under reconstruction in a U.N.-funded project.

Other Cities

Afghanistan's sixth-largest city, Jalalabad, sits at the base of the Khyber Pass, the last city in Afghanistan along the route to Peshawar, Pakistan. From the second to seventh centuries C.E., the area was a center of Buddhist culture, which fused with the Greek influence left by Alexander the Great. Jalalabad is famous for its oranges and as a winter resort. Because of its proximity to the border, it has served as headquarters for many aid organizations assisting Afghan refugees.

Ghazni is the capital of Ghazni Province and the only walled town remaining in Afghanistan. It flourished as a center of Islamic culture under the Ghaznavids (994–1160 C.E.), Afghanistan's first Muslim dynasty. The great Ghaznavid ruler Mahmud built a magnificent mosque known as the Celestial Bride there. The walled, old city of Ghazni is home to Mahmud's tomb. Located on the Kabul-Kandahar Highway, Ghazni is a trading center for sheep, wool, camel hair cloth, and fruit and is famous for its embroidered sheepskin coats.

Balkh is today only a small town, but it is known as the birthplace of Zoroaster. It was also an intellectual center of early Islam, considered by the Arabs as "the Mother of Cities." Genghis Khan devastated Balkh, and it never fully recovered. In 1866, after an outbreak of cholera, most residents of the city left. Several notable historical monuments still exist in Balkh, however, including the nine-domed Haji Piyada Mosque, and the Shrine of Khwaja Abu Nasr Parsa, an octagonal mosque with twisted columns, minarets, and a fluted blue dome.

Iranian president Mohammad Khatami (left) speaks with Hamid Karzai during the latter's 2002 visit to Tehran. Since the fall of the Taliban government, relations between Afghanistan and Iran have improved, although some areas of tension remain.

7

Foreign Relations

Afghanistan's relations with foreign powers, both regional and global, have since ancient times been affected by its strategic location on key trade routes and its vulnerability to invasion. After it was founded as an independent nation in 1747, Afghanistan became a pawn in the Great Game between Great Britain and Russia. During the Cold War era, Afghanistan received aid from both the United States and the Soviet Union, and in the 1980s it was the site of a proxy war between the two opposing superpowers. More recently, it was the focus of international attention because of the Taliban's very strict Islamic form of government, violations of human rights, and support for terrorist groups.

However, since the fall of the Taliban, Afghanistan has emerged on the world stage with its first real hope for peace since the late 1970s. Though the drug trade, warlords, and terrorism continue to threaten the country's security, it is working closely with the U.N. and many individual donor nations to return Afghan refugees to their homes; establish a stable, democratically elected government; rebuild the country's infrastructure and economy; and decrease poverty.

Foreign Relations into the Late 20th Century

In the 19th century, Afghanistan was treated as a buffer state between Russia to the north and the British-dominated Indian subcontinent. But in the 20th century, it depended on aid from the world's two new superpowers, the Soviet Union and the United States. The Soviet Union signed a friendship pact with Afghanistan in 1921, and between 1954 and 1978, it gave the country along its southwestern border more than $1.5 billion in economic and military aid. The United States formally established diplomatic relations with Afghanistan in 1934 and from 1950 to 1979 provided more than $500 million in non-military government aid. By the time the Soviets invaded in 1979, over a third of Afghanistan's total expenditures were financed by foreign aid.

During the 20th century, Afghanistan experienced recurrent problems with its eastern neighbor, Pakistan, and its western neighbor, Iran. Tensions with Pakistan centered on the Pashtun tribes living on both sides of the Durand Line, which since 1893 has formed Afghanistan's eastern boundary. Pashtun unrest led to numerous tribal uprisings, along with military campaigns to suppress them, first by the British and then by the Paskistani forces. Afghanistan's central problem with Iran was an ongoing dispute over the flow of the Helmand River into Iran, which Afghanistan sought to regulate.

The Soviet Occupation

After Communists seized power in Afghanistan in 1978, the United States and most other Western countries maintained a small diplomatic presence in Kabul. The U.S. embassy drastically reduced its staff after Ambassador Adolph Dubs was kidnapped and then killed in a shoot-out in February 1979. When, in December of that year, the Soviet Union invaded Afghanistan in support of the Communist regime, the United States responded by closing its mission in Kabul and ending all aid to the country. Other nations followed suit.

While the United States supported various diplomatic initiatives to effect a Soviet withdrawal from Afghanistan, it (along with Saudi Arabia and other countries) also provided covert military assistance to the mujahedin in their armed struggle against the Soviet occupation. Pakistan was key to these efforts, serving as a base for training resistance forces and as a conduit for U.S. arms. (With aid from the United States and other nations, Pakistan also supported the estimated 3 million Afghan refugees who had crossed its border from Afghanistan.) In addition, Pakistan led diplomatic opposition to the invasion in the United Nations, the **Non-Aligned Movement** (NAM), and the Organization of the Islamic Conference (OIC).

Iran also reacted strongly against the Soviet invasion of Afghanistan, even though its relations with the United States had by this time become extremely poor (largely because of the seizure of the U.S. embassy in Tehran and the holding of embassy staff hostage). Iran, which branded the Soviet Union "the Lesser Satan"—in contrast to the United States, "the Great Satan"—provided financial and military aid to Afghan mujahedin who advocated the kind of Islamic Revolution that swept Iran in 1979. Iran also became home to approximately 2 million refugees during the Soviet occupation.

A mujahedin in the Safed Koh Mountains aims a U.S.-made Stinger missile at a Soviet aircraft. During the 1979–1989 Soviet occupation, the U.S. government provided a great deal of military aid to the Afghan resistance.

The Rise of the Taliban

After the 1988 Geneva Accords, in which the Soviet Union agreed to leave Afghanistan, the Communist Afghan government attempted to reconcile Afghanistan to the Non-Aligned Movement and the Organization of the Islamic Conference, without success. The U.N. tried to put together a transitional government acceptable to both the Communists and the mujahedin, but the United States and its allies abandoned the peace process, and the U.N.'s efforts suffered as international donors turned their energies to other humanitarian crises. From the time the Northern Alliance of mujahedin groups took control of Kabul until the Taliban wrested it away from them in 1996, little international attention focused on Afghanistan.

Many members of the Taliban were born in Afghan refugee camps in northwestern Pakistan, where they were then educated in fundamentalist madrassas and trained as mujahedin. They were Sunni Muslims and also Pashtuns, like the Pakistanis among whom they lived. Pakistan thus became a primary backer of the Taliban. By providing money, training, and equipment to the Taliban, Pakistan hoped to bring some stability to its war-torn neighbor while developing Afghanistan as a close ally in its ongoing disputes with India.

However, the Taliban were highly unpopular with neighboring Iran, which was alarmed by the regime's brutal treatment of Afghanistan's Shia minority (Iran's population is overwhelmingly Shiite). Following the execution of eight Iranian diplomats in Mazar-e-Sharif in 1998 and the Taliban's decision to shut off all flow of the Helmand River into Iran in 1999, Iran increased its assistance to the Northern Alliance.

The United States, which had supported the Taliban through its close ally Pakistan, initially looked to the Taliban to rid Afghanistan of terrorist training camps and opium smuggling and to stabilize the country for open trade. The United States was also interested in the American oil company UNOCAL's plans to develop a pipeline from the oil-rich Central Asian countries through Afghanistan to Pakistan, a move that would divert the oil trade away from U.S. enemy Iran. U.S. openness to the Taliban did not, however, last long.

Meanwhile, Russia and members of the Commonwealth of Independent States (CIS), an alliance of many of the former Soviet republics, began to have their own concerns about the Taliban. Because the Taliban was providing a sanctuary for terrorist groups active in Russia and Central Asia, Russia gave military assistance to the Northern Alliance.

The Taliban regime showed little understanding of international diplomacy or the politics of other nations. And whenever international law or international organizations conflicted with the Taliban's view of Islamic government, the Taliban simply ignored them. As a result, the Taliban experienced almost complete isolation from the world community. Only Pakistan, Saudi Arabia, and the United Arab Emirates recognized the Taliban regime. With Pakistan's help, the Taliban repeatedly attempted to occupy Afghanistan's seat at the U.N. and OIC, but it was always rejected. The U.N. continued to call for peaceful negotiations to establish a broad-based, multiethnic, democratic government, but the Taliban remained uncooperative.

International opposition to the Taliban gradually coalesced, hinging on five issues: terrorist training activity, burgeoning opium production, the rights of women, the exploding population of Afghan refugees, and the treatment of international aid agencies. The world community, led by the United States, grew increasingly concerned about al-Qaeda's terrorist activity and its friendly relations with the Taliban. From 1991 to 1996, al-Qaeda was based in Sudan. After being expelled from Sudan in 1996, however, bin Laden moved the group's base of operations and training camps to Afghanistan. Al-Qaeda became the chief suspect in the August 1998 bombings of U.S. embassies in Kenya and Tanzania, and the United States retaliated with cruise missile strikes against al-Qaeda terrorist training camps in eastern Afghanistan. The missile strikes seem only to have solidified al-Qaeda's relationship with the Taliban, however.

Under the Taliban, Afghanistan also became the world's largest opium producer, and nations around the world grew increasingly concerned about drug trafficking. The Taliban wanted to earn revenue from opium smuggling without alienating foreign governments, but found it difficult to strike this balance. In 1998 approximately 96 percent of the country's total opium cultivation occurred in provinces under Taliban control. In 2000 the Taliban ordered a total ban on poppy cultivation, but the regime already had large stockpiles of opium ready for smuggling.

Meanwhile, after the Taliban began enforcing strict rules on women's behavior, international women's groups started pressuring their governments to respond. Following the United Nations Fourth World Conference on Women, held in Beijing in 1995, women's groups successfully lobbied the international community to reject Taliban requests to occupy Afghanistan's U.N. seat. They also protested UNOCAL's proposed oil pipeline through Afghanistan, prompting the company to terminate its plans. The pressure only grew after the Taliban detained the European Union commissioner for humanitarian affairs, Emma Bonino, in 1997, and after U.S. secretary of state Madeleine Albright called Taliban treatment of women "despicable."

The Taliban also showed disregard for international humanitarian aid groups attempting to address the health and refugee crises in Afghanistan. In the mid-1990s, the country had only one functioning hospital for every 500,000 people in some areas, and disease rates were on the rise. By the mid-1990s, the Red Crescent Society (the equivalent of the Red Cross in

Taliban justice was draconian. These two Afghan rebels were publicly hanged in Kabul; in other cases Afghans who dissented or were suspected of being criminals were flogged or had their hands cut off. The Taliban's disregard for good relations with its neighbors, and its willingness to shelter terrorists like Osama bin Laden, alienated much of the world.

Muslim countries) and other relief agencies were working inside the country. However, after the Taliban governor of Kandahar Province assaulted a U.N. staffer in 1998, the United Nations suspended its humanitarian activities throughout southern Afghanistan, and following the U.S. cruise missile strikes on terrorist training camps in 1998, the U.N. and other groups withdrew from the country completely.

After September 11

The terrorist attacks of September 11, 2001, immediately made Afghanistan the focus of international attention. The U.S. government identified al-Qaeda as the chief suspect in the attacks, but Taliban leader Mullah Muhammad Omar refused to surrender bin Laden, despite numerous U.N. Security Council resolutions that his country do so as well as pressure from Pakistan. Saudi Arabia and the United Arab Emirates then withdrew their recognition of the Taliban, and Pakistan closed its border with Afghanistan.

The United States built an international coalition for a war to oust the Taliban and roll up the al-Qaeda terrorists the regime was harboring. Pakistan opened up its air space and bases for use by the coalition, and on October 7, 2001, U.S. and British forces launched massive air strikes against al-Qaeda and Taliban bases in Afghanistan. After a sustained bombing campaign, the Northern Alliance, supported by the coalition, advanced toward Kabul. By December the Taliban had been routed.

With the fall of the Taliban and the institution of the newly created Islamic Republic of Afghanistan, the country once again became an active member of the international community and reestablished diplomatic relations with countries around the world. In December 2002, the six countries that border Afghanistan—China, Pakistan, Iran, Turkmenistan, Uzbekistan, and Tajikistan—signed the Kabul Declaration on Good Neighborly Relations, in which they pledged to respect Afghanistan's independence and territorial integrity.

Countries from around the world have also pledged financial aid for the rebuilding of Afghanistan. At a meeting in Tokyo, Japan, in January 2002, more than 60 countries, together with development institutions and non-governmental organizations, pledged in excess of $4.5 billion in aid to Afghanistan. Not all of these pledges were met, however, and President Hamid Karzai asked a second donors' conference, held in Bonn, Germany, in March 2004, for $27 billion. Approximately $8.2 billion was pledged. The largest donor at both conferences was the United States. Afghanistan and the International Monetary Fund agreed in June 2006 on an additional program for 2006–2009, focusing on reducing poverty and boosting growth and stability.

Representing the United States, former Secretary of State Colin Powell spoke at the International Conference on Reconstruction Assistance to Afghanistan, held January 2002 in Tokyo. More than $4.5 billion in aid was pledged at the conference, but the Afghan government complained that donor countries were slow to deliver the promised funds.

Since the fall of the Taliban, the U.N. has helped Afghan refugees return to their homes, supervised mine-clearing projects, and provided health care, educational programs, and food. The U.N. also oversaw the organization of the 2004 national elections.

Afghanistan and Pakistan have been working to improve their relationship. This is important for the future of both countries, since much of Afghanistan still relies on Pakistan for trade and travel connections to the rest of the world, and Pakistan hopes Afghanistan will eventually become its primary transportation route for trade with Central Asia in exchange for the construction of vital energy links. Up to 2 million Afghan refugees still live in Pakistan.

Afghanistan's relations with Iran have also improved, though tensions linger. As of 2004, up to 2 million Afghan refugees were still living in Iran; as many as 400,000 of them came from southwestern Afghanistan, which turned into desert after the Taliban stopped the flow of the Helmand River to Iran. Iran has pledged money to Afghan reconstruction efforts, particularly in the western portion of the country, and is constructing a road between its eastern border and Herat, a major trade route linking the two countries. Nevertheless, since Afghanistan has been plagued by drought and needs the water from the Helmand River, struggles over its flow into Iran are ongoing.

The new government of Afghanistan has worked to improve relations with Russia, but bitterness persists over the brutality of the Soviet occupation. Afghanistan's outstanding foreign debt to Russia is another ongoing source of conflict. Nevertheless, in an effort to expand trade relations, the two countries are planning a second bridge over the Amu Darya River, which runs along the border between Afghanistan and its Central Asian neighbors.

The chief interest of the United States in Afghanistan is to support a democratically elected representative government that helps provide regional stability, is open to free trade, and respects human rights. U.S. non-military aid (over $12 billion between the years of 2001–2006) is used for clearing land mines, reconstruction, and humanitarian assistance. But, in the wake of the U.S. occupation of Iraq in 2003, Muslim nations have warned that the continuing involvement of the United States in Afghanistan could come at a price, as citizens throughout the Muslim world increasingly resent what they see as Western interference in the affairs of sovereign nations.

Afghanistan's relations with other countries highlight the critical issues that continue to affect its prospects for a peaceful future. Post-2001 al-Qaeda attacks in Saudi Arabia, Spain, Pakistan, and Yemen, among other

Afghan National Army recruits practice saluting in their new uniforms at a training site in Kabul. Although Afghan military and police forces are being trained to assume the security duties in their country, experts expect U.S. troops to remain in Afghanistan indefinitely to help protect the government, curb the activities of regional warlords, and disrupt terrorist activities.

places, have only reinforced for the United States and its allies the importance of preventing Afghanistan from once again devolving into a haven for radical Islamic terrorists. Yet even after Afghanistan's successful democratic elections, much work remained to be done before the country had quashed the threat of terrorism and other dangers to its stability and security. President Karzai himself has said that the drug trade, warlordism, and terrorism all reinforce one another. In early 2004, Afghanistan and its neighbors signed an anti-drug accord in which they pledged to stop the illegal opium trade by tightening control at the borders and arresting drug traffickers. Yet several years later, a bumper crop of opium poppy had been harvested, Taliban remnants continued to mount periodic attacks in southern Afghanistan and even to kidnap U.N. workers, Osama bin Laden and Mullah Muhammad Omar remained at large, and well-armed and -financed warlords continued to operate largely beyond the authority of the central government. Clearly Afghanistan had a long way to go to secure a peaceful and prosperous future for its citizens.

500 B.C.E.	Darius the Great extends the Persian Empire into Afghanistan.
329 B.C.E.	Alexander the Great establishes Greek rule in Persia and Afghanistan.
400–652	The Persian Sassanid dynasty, the Ephthalites, and the Turkish tribes of Central Asia struggle for control.
651	Arabs conquer the important cities Herat and Balkh and bring the first contact with Islam.
962–1140	The Ghaznavid dynasty establishes Afghanistan as a center of Islamic civilization.
1504	Babur invades and rules the Mughal dynasty from Kabul.
1736	Nadir Shah of Persia occupies Afghanistan.
1747	Ahmad Shah unifies modern-day Afghanistan and becomes the country's first king.
1839–42	The First Anglo-Afghan War is fought principally because of Britain's determination to maintain Afghanistan as a buffer state with Russia.
1878–80	The Second Anglo-Afghan War culminates in withdrawal by the British.
1919	Afghanistan reestablishes its sovereignty after the very brief Third Anglo-Afghan War; this status is confirmed by the amended Treaty of Riwalpindi (1921).
1919–29	Radical reforms occur under King Amanullah.
1933	Zahir Shah becomes Afghanistan's last king.
1934	The United States formally recognizes Afghanistan.
1953	General Muhammad Daoud becomes prime minister and turns to the Soviet Union for economic and military aid.
1963	Daoud is forced to resign as prime minister.
1964	A new constitution establishes a constitutional monarchy, but the government steadily weakens.
1973	Daoud overthrows King Zahir Shah in a military coup; the Republic of Afghanistan is established.
1978	The Communist People's Democratic Party of Afghanistan (PDPA) leads the Saur Revolution, which overthrows Daoud.
1979	In December the Soviet Union invades Afghanistan in support of the Communist regime.

Chronology

1980	The Soviets install Babrak Karmal as ruler, but mujahedin groups increase their resistance with backing from the United States, Pakistan, and other countries.
1989	The Soviet Union fully withdraws from Afghanistan, but the mujahedin seek to oust the Communist government.
1993	The mujahedin agree on a new government with Burhanuddin Rabbani as president.
1996	The Taliban take control of Kabul and enforce a strict version of Islamic law.
1997	The Taliban control about two-thirds of the country.
1999	The U.N. imposes sanctions on the Taliban and demands that al-Qaeda leader Osama bin Laden be handed over for trial.
2001	In October the United States and Britain quickly defeat the Taliban after they refuse to hand over Osama bin Laden, chief suspect in the September 11 terrorist attacks on New York and Washington, D.C.; in December Hamid Karzai is sworn in as head of an interim government.
2002	In June a loya jirga elects Hamid Karzai president of the Transitional Islamic State of Afghanistan (TISA).
2004	In January a loya jirga adopts a new constitution; Hamid Karzai is elected president in Afghanistan's first democratic election, held in October.
2005	Parliamentary elections are held in September, and the Parliament meets for the first time in 30 years.
2006	NATO assumes responsibility for security across Afghanistan, taking command in the east from a US-led coalition force.
2007	Afghan and Pakistani troops clash violently in the worst border dispute in decades. Former king Zahir Shah dies.
2008	At a conference in Paris, Western governments commit $20 billion more in aid to Afghanistan. The Taliban free at least 350 insurgents from Kandahar prison. President Karzai accuses Afghan and US-led forces of killing at least 89 civilians in an air strike in the province of Herat.

arable—capable of being farmed productively.

bazaar—an area of small shops and people selling various goods.

buffer state—a neutral nation located between two rival powers.

caliphate—the dominion of the chief Muslim ruler, who is regarded as a successor of Muhammad.

constitutional monarchy—a monarchy in which the powers of the ruler are restricted to those granted under the nation's constitution and laws.

fundamentalist—relating or belonging to a movement or trend that stresses strict and literal adherence to a set of basic principles; in religion, an advocate of efforts to purify the religion by laying out its fundamentals and expecting adherence to them.

gross domestic product (GDP)—the total value of all goods and services produced within a country during a one-year period.

Hadith—a narrative record of the sayings and customs of the prophet Muhammad and his companions.

karez—an irrigation system, developed about 3,000 years ago in Iran, that taps groundwater supplies through sloping tunnels using gravity flow.

land reform—the redistribution of the agricultural resources of a country, usually to expropriate land that is concentrated in the hands of a small group of people and redistribute it among small farmers and farming cooperatives.

muezzin—the mosque official who summons faithful Muslims to prayer five times each day.

Muslim Brotherhood—an Islamic organization that opposes the secular tendencies of Islamic nations, rejects Western influences, and advocates a return to the precepts of the Qur'an.

mystical—relating to or concerning mysticism, the belief that one can experience direct union with the divine, especially through prayer and meditation; more generally, relating to an emphasis in religion on feeling and faith rather than reason.

Glossary

nationalism—a collective consciousness in which citizens emphasize the culture, interests, and political independence of their nation.

Non-Aligned Movement (NAM)—an international organization consisting of more than 100 nations that consider themselves not to be formally aligned with or against a global superpower.

oligarchy—a form of government in which most political power rests in the hands of a small segment of society.

patrilineal—based on or tracing descent through the male line.

polygyny—the custom of having more than one wife at a time.

polytheism—the belief in more than one god.

Shia—the second-largest branch of Islam, based on the belief that members of Muhammad's family were the rightful successors to the Prophet.

Sikh—an adherent of Sikhism, a monotheistic religion founded in the 15th century, with similarities to both Islam and Hinduism.

steppe—a vast semiarid grass-covered plain.

Sunni—the majority branch of Islam, which accepts the first four caliphs as rightful successors to Muhammad.

theocracy—a form of government in which laws and policies are either identical with or strongly influenced by the principles of a particular religion.

Wahhabism—an Islamic fundamentalist movement founded in 18th-century Arabia and now influential particularly in Saudi Arabia.

warlord—a leader who controls a particular area of a country through military power, usually when the central government is weak.

yurt—a circular, domed, portable dwelling, common among nomads in central Asia.

Zoroastrianism—a religious system founded by Zoroaster and set forth in the holy text the Aveta, which teaches the worship of a single God in the context of a universal struggle between good and evil; it was at various times the national religion of Persia (ancient Iran).

Further Reading

Armstrong, Karen. *Islam: A Short History.* New York: Modern Library, 2000.

Chayes, Sarah. *The Punishment of Virtue: Inside Afghanistan After the Taliban.* New York: The Penguin Press, 2006.

Cooley, John K. *Unholy Wars: Afghanistan, America and International Terrorism.* London: Pluto Press, 2002.

Cristofari, Rita, and John Follain. *Zoya's Story: An Afghan Woman's Struggle for Freedom.* New York: Perennial, 2003.

Elliot, Jason. *An Unexpected Light: Travels in Afghanistan.* New York: Picador, 2001.

Ewans, Martin. *Afghanistan: A Short History of Its People and Politics.* New York: HarperCollins, 2002.

Hauner, Milan, and Robert Canfield (eds.). *Afghanistan and the Soviet Union: Collision and Transformation.* Boulder, Colo.: Westview Press, 1989.

Hopkirk, Peter. *The Great Game: The Struggle for Empire in Central Asia.* New York: Kodansha International, 1994.

Kakar, M. Hassan. *Afghanistan: The Soviet Invasion and the Afghan Response, 1979–1982.* Berkeley: University of California Press, 1997.

Kremmer, Christopher. *The Carpet Wars: From Kabul to Baghdad: A Ten-Year Journey Along Ancient Trade Routes.* New York: Ecco, 2002.

Lamb, Christina. *The Sewing Circles of Herat: A Personal Voyage Through Afghanistan.* New York: HarperCollins, 2002.

Omrani, Bijan, and Matthew Leeming. *Afghanistan: A Companion and Guide, Revised Edition.* New York: Odyssey Books, 2007.

Rashid, Ahmed. *Taliban: Militant Islam, Oil and Fundamentalism in Central Asia.* New Haven, Conn.: Yale University Press, 2001.

http://www.afghanistannews.net

Up-to-the-minute news from Afghanistan, with links to archived news articles.

http://www.afghanmagazine.com/

Independent online magazine focusing on the arts and culture of Afghanistan.

http://www.un.org/apps/news/infocusRel1.asp?infocusID=16&Body=Afghanistan

Comprehensive news on U.N. assistance in Afghanistan, including a history of Afghanistan's role in the U.N.

http://www.lib.berkeley.edu/SSEAL/SouthAsia/afghan_US.html

Comprehensive collection of Internet resources on Afghanistan and the United States.

http://www.cnn.com/SPECIALS/2001/taliban/

In-depth exploration of the Taliban movement and government.

http://www.academicinfo.net/afghanwomen.html

Comprehensive collection of Internet resources on women in Afghanistan.

Numbers in **bold italic** refer to captions.

Index

Picture Credits

Contributors

The **FOREIGN POLICY RESEARCH INSTITUTE (FPRI)** served as editorial consultants for the MAJOR MUSLIM NATIONS series. FPRI is one of the nation's oldest "think tanks." The Institute's Middle East Program focuses on Gulf security, monitors the Arab-Israeli peace process, and sponsors an annual conference for teachers on the Middle East, plus periodic briefings on key developments in the region.

Among the FPRI's trustees is a former Secretary of State and a former Secretary of the Navy (and among the FPRI's former trustees and interns, two current Undersecretaries of Defense), not to mention two university presidents emeritus, a foundation president, and several active or retired corporate CEOs.

The scholars of FPRI include a former aide to three U.S. Secretaries of State, a Pulitzer Prize–winning historian, a former president of Swarthmore College and a Bancroft Prize–winning historian, and two former staff members of the National Security Council. And the FPRI counts among its extended network of scholars—especially its Inter-University Study Groups—representatives of diverse disciplines, including political science, history, economics, law, management, religion, sociology, and psychology.

DR. HARVEY SICHERMAN is president and director of the Foreign Policy Research Institute in Philadelphia, Pennsylvania. He has extensive experience in writing, research, and analysis of U.S. foreign and national security policy, both in government and out. He served as Special Assistant to Secretary of State Alexander M. Haig Jr. and as a member of the Policy Planning Staff of Secretary of State James A. Baker III. Dr. Sicherman was also a consultant to Secretary of the Navy John F. Lehman Jr. (1982–1987) and Secretary of State George Shultz (1988).

A graduate of the University of Scranton (B.S., History, 1966), Dr. Sicherman earned his Ph.D. at the University of Pennsylvania (Political Science, 1971), where he received a Salvatori Fellowship. He is author or editor of numerous books and articles, including *America the Vulnerable: Our Military Problems and How to Fix Them* (FPRI, 2002) and *Palestinian Autonomy, Self-Government and Peace* (Westview Press, 1993). He edits *Peacefacts*, an FPRI bulletin that monitors the Arab-Israeli peace process.

KIM WHITEHEAD is a writer and professor living in Mississippi. She specializes in religion, women's studies, and contemporary literature and has written two books on Islam. She received her Ph.D. from the Institute of Liberal Arts at Emory University.